Mastering
Swaps Markets

market editions

Mastering Swaps Markets

A step-by-step guide to the
products, applications and risks

ALAN McDOUGALL

PEARSON EDUCATION LIMITED

Head Office:
Edinburgh Gate
Harlow CM20 2JE
Tel: +44 (0)1279 623623
Fax: +44 (0)1279 431059

London Office:
128 Long Acre, London WC2E 9AN
Tel: +44 (0)171 447 2000
Fax: +44 (0)171 240 5771
www.business-minds.com

———————————

First published in Great Britain 1999

ISBN 0 273 62588 8

British Library Cataloguing in Publication Data
A CIP catalogue record for this book can be obtained from the British Library.

10 9 8 7 6 5 4 3 2 1

Typeset by Northern Phototypesetting Co. Ltd, Bolton.
Printed and bound in Great Britain by Redwood Books, Trowbridge, Wiltshire.

The Publishers' policy is to use paper manufactured from sustainable forests.

About the Author

Alan McDougall is a consultant and trainer in international finance, specializing in the relationship between the swap, foreign exchange and bond markets.

He joined Kleinwort Benson as a credit analyst, focusing on Asian credits, before being offered the opportunity to train as a foreign exchange and money market trader, working in both the forward and depo markets. He became the senior consultant at HSBC's International Treasury Management Group where he worked with multinational corporations in the management of their currency and interest rate risk exposures which often included the use of swap transactions. He subsequently ran the swaps and capital markets arbitrage group at Nikko Europe and was Vice President Illiquid bond trading at Scotia Capital Markets before becoming a full-time researcher, consultant and trainer.

Alan ran his first training session over 20 years ago and he has combined his experience of trading and sales with his enthusiasm for teaching and consulting throughout his career.

He has run training course for banks, investment banks, corporations, fund managers and software houses on the following subjects:

- the practical applications of bond mathematics
- understanding the practicalities of bond and fixed income markets
- pricing and hedging swaps
- advanced bond trading techniques
- the international capital markets
- mastering the foreign exchange and money markets
- relating bond and swap spreads: an approach for traders
- interest rate risk management
- advanced swap techniques
- the European high yield bond markets
- OTC derivatives
- bond sales and trading workshop
- treasury risk management
- credit derivatives
- understanding the capital markets
- an introduction to investment banking
- financial ratios for fund managers
- the international financial markets.

If you would like more information about these training courses please contact Alan McDougall by telephone 44 181 444 3668,
e-mail alan@capitalmarkets.demon.co.uk,
or write to him at 16 Landsdowne Road, London N10 2AU.

CONTENTS

Contents

To Liisa, Duncan and Hamish,
whom I wouldn't swap for the world.

FOREWORD

Swaps are an integral part of the world of international finance. Their use has permeated almost every aspect of domestic and international capital and money markets. Banks use them to reduce their exposure to the risk of changes in interest rates and currency movements, thereby reducing the potential tax burden on the public which results from the failure of banks. Many governments use swaps as a tool to reduce the cost of international funding. This also helps to reduce the general tax burden. The existence of swaps creates greater choice for consumers in the provision of fixed-rate finance for mortgages, or even of loans with caps or other embedded options.

The arbitrage opportunities which are capitalized in the swap market have resulted in a narrowing of the capital markets bid/offer spread. This means that institutional investors get a better return on their investments and international borrowers pay lower financing costs. This, in turn, results in more competitively priced goods for consumers and in enhanced returns for pensioners. Swaps therefore have an effect on almost all of us yet they remain an arcane derivatives risk management tool, sometimes suspected of providing the international banking system with the tools required to bring about its destruction.

This book traces the development of swaps from the 1970s until today, examining the obstacles to their growth and the hurdles which were jumped in order to ensure their survival. It shows how swaps are used, and by whom, and examines the motives of the counterparties to these transactions as well as the resultant benefits. The exercises and case studies are designed to help readers understand the practical applications of swaps as well as the maths used in the marketplace. All the financial calculations are broken down in a step by step process designed to help those who prefer to see numbers rather than formulae.

The book is aimed at those who work in the financial markets and have regular dealings with the swap markets. This includes traders, salespeople, operational staff, brokers, risk managers, borrowers, investors, auditors, accountants, lawyers, senior managers, IT staff and all those who sell to banks and investment banks and who require a better understanding of their clients' businesses.

The book assumes no prior knowledge of the swaps market and a dedicated reader willing to work through the exercises and case studies will become proficient in the major applications of currency and interest rate swaps, as well as the mathematical techniques employed in arranging, structuring and valuing swaps. The book can also be used by market practitioners who need to explore in detail one aspect of the swap market. Borrowers, investors or arrangers, for example, who need to extend their knowledge of the maths involved in the new issue arbitrage process could use the book to accomplish this.

Readers could use this book as a complete study course in swap market techniques by answering the questions in the text. Alternatively, by reading the text and skimming the exercises the book can be used as a guide to the functioning of the swap market. It can also be used as a reference tool for particular swap market techniques.

ACKNOWLEDGEMENTS

This book is based on ideas generated by teaching swaps to my colleagues and clients since 1981. I would like to thank all of them for the part their questions played in helping me to develop my understanding of the swap market well enough to write about it. Kevin Regan, Aiden Frayne, Andrew Ruffell and Heather Schemilt stand out amongst many whose inquisitiveness contributed to the development of my skills as a teacher.

I am very grateful to David Pinchin for encouraging me and coaching me as a public speaker, Sue Lovell-Greene for her determination and perseverance in helping me to write and deliver my first swaps training course and Jane Lewis for providing an inexhaustible supply of eager and enthusiastic swaps traders, salespeople and many others for me to teach.

I am also grateful to Bob Steiner who suggested this book to me, initially as a joint venture, and then as a solo project. He wrote two books while I was thinking about this one and encouraged me to believe that I might follow in his footsteps.

I received great encouragement while writing this book, particularly from my wife Liisa and from my parents. I am also especially grateful to Richard Stagg, Jeff Hearn, Orla Holland, Sarah Worthington, Sue Lovell-Greene, Jane Lewis, Jo Byrne, Petros Gerulanos, Richard Capps, Linda Dhondy and Andrew Ruffell who each made a special contribution to the production of this book.

An Introduction to the Swap Markets

How swaps developed

Treasury and capital market products

Too good to last?

Capital adequacy

Overview

This chapter traces the development of the early market in swaps and explains the significance of the much-publicized deal between IBM and the World Bank. It goes on to discuss the suspicion with which swaps were regarded by many in the financial markets and the importance of a single legal agreement in the structuring of swaps. It charts the formation of the International Swap Dealers Association and explains its role, particularly the importance of standard documentation for swap contracts. It goes on to discuss the pioneering of swap warehousing by Citibank and explains some of the factors which were responsible for the dramatic growth in the swap markets and the reactions of the international financial regulators to this exposive growth.

How swaps developed

The first interest rate swap was transacted in 1981 between Deutsche Bank and an undisclosed counterparty. Currency swaps – brought into prominence in the same year by an article in the *Wall Street Journal* about a deal Salomon Brothers International arranged between IBM and the International Bank for Reconstruction and Development (the World Bank) – had been in existence for some years in a variety of forms including parallel and back-to-back loans.

These transactions were often used as a means of avoiding, but not evading, exchange control regulations. Since there was no actual sale of sterling involved in these structures, there was no reason for the Bank of England to object to them. For example, if Shell wanted to make a loan to one of its US subsidiaries prior to the abolition of exchange control regulations in the United Kingdom in October 1979, then the required sale of sterling and purchase of US dollars would have incurred a premium which would have made the cost of the loan uneconomic. If on the other hand Shell, for example, made a loan in sterling to a US company's UK subsidiary, and the US company made a loan in dollars to, say, Shell's US subsidiary, there would be no need for either party to pay the investment premium.

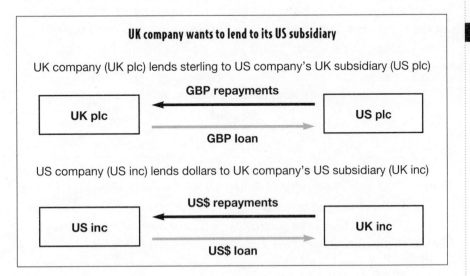

UK company wants to lend to its US subsidiary

UK company (UK plc) lends sterling to US company's UK subsidiary (US plc)

GBP repayments

UK plc   US plc

GBP loan

US company (US inc) lends dollars to UK company's US subsidiary (UK inc)

US$ repayments

US inc   UK inc

US$ loan

Fig 1.1

While the loans resulting from this technique were more likely to be at competitive market prices for the borrowers, they suffered from a legal drawback. The sterling loan would usually be governed by English Law while the dollar loan might be governed by New York Law. There would therefore be no automatic right of set-off. So if the US company's UK subsidiary failed to repay the sterling loan there would be no automatic right for the UK company's US subsidiary to offset the dollar loan against the sterling loan. The revolution that was about to occur in the derivatives market was given a tremendous boost when a structure was put in place whereby currency swaps could be transacted under a single legal agreement.

> **Swaps are transacted under a single legal agreement.**

The lack of a single legal agreement, and therefore the absence of a right of offset, was not the only barrier to the early development of the swap market. Each of the market participants had a different legal contract under which their institution would arrange swaps. If two parties wanted to arrange a deal, then it was usual for them to meet in order to discuss the legal preferences of their institution. While this might only be done once for each new counterparty, it was still a fairly time-consuming and inefficient way in which to do business.

Swaps were also regarded with a good deal of suspicion by some of the prospective counterparties. To some extent this was because the avoidance of regulation was involved and the distinction between the legal status of avoidance and evasion is not always apparent. A good deal of the skepticism came from the "zero sum game" school of thought – if I am winning in a transaction then you must be losing. Two popular city expressions encapsulate this idea:

> *"If you don't know who is losing money in a transaction then*
> *it's you!"*

> *"If it looks too good to be true then it probably is."*

Not many were propounding Ricardo's ideas that everybody could be better off if only they exploited their strengths rather than chased their needs. In currency and interest rate terms this translates into companies borrowing what they are comparatively best at borrowing and swapping into the exposure which best suits their preferred risk profile.

But a great deal of the resistance to swaps stemmed from the fact that they seemed rather complicated to the prospective users in the early 1980s. It took a good deal of determination and a fair amount of time to structure a swap then, and from a personal risk management perspective, there would often have appeared to be more downside than upside potential in getting involved in the swap market. Even those who took the plunge and made a decision that it was worth investing management time were confronted with another obstacle. No bank made a market in swaps. All transactions were arranged on a matched basis. This meant that if a company wanted to swap from fixed-rate Swedish krone to fixed-rate US dollars, it was necessary to find a counterparty willing to do the opposite transaction. This might take two days, or two weeks, and of course the currency and interest rate exposures which had been earmarked for hedging would remain open during the time taken to find a counterparty. Clearly this is rather different from the market today where two parties can close a deal in a matter of seconds and settle the trade with a standard confirmation and pre-agreed, standardized legal documentation.

The formation of the International Swap Dealers Association (ISDA) in 1984 was an attempt, amongst other things, to speed up the growth of the market by standardizing swap documentation. In 1983 some banks introduced policies under which they declined to deal with counterparties with whom documentation was outstanding for more than, say, six months after a trade had taken place. While administratively and procedurally these policies were admirable they did little to encourage volumes and the development of a liquid market.

When ISDA produced a standard legal agreement in 1985 it was a significant boost for the market. In addition to the benefits of administrative efficiencies banks were also reassured that the marketplace was now operating under a common standard. This significantly reduced the risk that one bank would have a legal advantage over another as a result of superior documentation and resulted in the marketplace as a whole having a common pool and a common interest in legal improvements to the contractual aspects of swaps. The British Bankers Association also made a significant contribution to the development of the market with the publication of their interest rate swap terms, or BBAIRS terms, as they are known in the market.

While banks searched for counterparties with matching interests to those of their swap clients there was, in addition to the currency and interest rate risk run by the client, a competitive risk for the bank. Many customers indicated their hedging intentions to a variety of banks so there was often a number of houses searching for the same counterparty. Apart from the price effects of this, banks were also aware that their lack of ability to deal at the time the customer requested it often resulted in them losing the business to a rival firm.

Swap warehousing, or running mismatches, offered two immediate benefits. For the clients it meant that it was possible to cover an exposure almost as soon as the decision to do so was made. For the banks it meant that, subject to quoting the most competitive price, they would win their client's business. Even if they lost the business they were likely to do so with much less time invested in the counterparty matching process.

The growth of the swap markets was also fueled by the interest in the product of both treasury and capital markets players.

Treasury and capital market products

> At the birth of the swap markets, treasury and capital market products were two very distinct groups.

In 1980 it was reasonable to divide products into one category or the other. So bonds, for example, were considered to be a capital market instrument while spot and forward foreign exchange were considered to be treasury products. Bills and commercial paper were money market products and therefore belonged to the treasury group and once the time to maturity for a bond fell below one year it underwent a transformation from capital market instrument to money market product.

Traders, salespeople, arrangers, structurers and brokers were used to the idea of working in either the capital markets or the treasury area. Once the currency swap was developed there was, for the first time, a product which was of interest to both groups. In the early years of the swap market people from both a money market, or treasury background, and capital market professionals applied their skills to the development of the product.

The prospect of earning an arrangement fee of, say, 50 basis points from each party, plus an intermediation spread of, say, 1% per annum was enormously appealing to commercial, merchant and investment banks. The fact that many of the commercial banks had full balance sheets and the swap market provided a way to develop their off-balance sheet activities added considerably to the appeal.

> In the early years of the swap market, it was possible to charge a fee to each of the parties to a transaction.

Currency volatility was a major issue for many multinational corporations at this time and there were few possibilities for managing medium-term currency exposures during the 1970s, after the collapse of the Bretton Woods agreement and the floating of the US dollar and the D-mark. The oil price shocks of the 1970s contributed to great uncertainty about the outlook for interest rates. In the early 1980s US dollar rates rose from over 10% to almost 20% before declining and then shooting up again. Many companies which had been content to let their bankers worry about interest rates and exchange rates decided that they needed to take an active role in the management of these risks to their profits. The collapse of Laker Airways was attributed by some to the poor management of currency risk.

Once banks had decided to take positions in the currency swap market it became increasingly important to analyze the residual exposures on a mark-to-market basis and this task was greatly facilitated by the availability of the Apple Macintosh and the Excel spreadsheet. While it would have been possible to run a small book and perform many of these calculations on a financial calculator, it really took a spreadsheet to handle more than just a few deals. Financial calculators became widely used for pricing deals with almost universal acceptance of Hewlett Packard's 12C. Some years later a rumor spread in the market that Hewlett Packard was considering removing the 12C from its product range in favor of the more sophisticated 17Bs and 19Bs. There was such a surge in sales of the 12C, reputedly from swap traders buying themselves an extra one, that Hewlett Packard reversed their decision.

Too good to last?

It could be said that the circumstances of the early 1980s were perfect for the development of the swap market. Deregulation, volatility, competitive pressures, financial calculators, personal computers, spreadsheets, full balance sheets, the combination of money market and capital market methodologies, all were available to fuel the growth of the product. Swaps were of course not the only beneficiary of this wonderful confluence of positive factors. Financial futures enjoyed a boom after the first contract, a government backed mortgage future, was traded in Chicago in 1976. The London International Financial Futures Association was established in 1981. In the same year Citibank and Marine Midland, now part of the Hongkong Bank Group, pioneered the development of over-the-counter currency options and the first interest rate swap was arranged. Salomon

Brothers arranged a currency swap from US dollars to D-marks and Swiss francs for the World Bank and IBM. This transaction really caught the public eye. Given the suspicion with which many potential counterparties regarded swaps, the public approval of two AAA/Aaa rated entities – so well regarded in financial circles – was like a product endorsement. If swaps were a good idea for the World Bank and a good idea for IBM then surely others could benefit. Prior to the announcement of this deal in August 1981, only a very small number of the more sophisticated treasury managers at some of the major multinationals would have contemplated involving themselves in currency swaps. Now such swaps became fashionable.

The main concern at the time, and a subject which seemed to occupy the minds of many swap market participants, was whether swaps were too good to last. This was therefore a topic of concern to the members of ISDA. There would be little point in marketwide acceptance of a standard form of documentation if central banks and monetary authorities around the world decided to ban swaps, or restrict their use.

ISDA therefore had two initial objectives. The first was to act as a lobby to regulators to promote the benefits of swaps as a risk management tool and the second was to provide a service to the founder members, and any other market participant, by publishing a standard set of documentation. These objectives were set within an overall framework which was to promote good business practices in the swap market, encourage high standards of professionalism in the marketplace and increase public awareness and understanding of swaps.

These were the founder members of ISDA:

- Citibank
- Bankers Trust
- Morgan Stanley
- Morgan Guaranty
- First Boston
- Kleinwort Benson
- Goldman Sachs
- Merrill Lynch
- Salomon
- Sherson Lehman.

Liquidity in the swap markets was aided considerably by capital markets transactions, often involving swap driven new issues. While in absolute terms the proportion of swap driven deals was quite small, growing from about 5% of all new issues in 1983 to about 30% of new issues in 1987, there were a number of benefits to market participants. There was a regular flow of transactions to the marketplace as there was no shortage of borrowers willing to tap the markets to create floating-rate debt at sub-Libor levels of about 100 basis points. The credit arbitrages quickly reduced these opportunities so that by 1985 the sub-Libor spread had narrowed to 70–80 basis points, falling to about 30–40 basis points in 1999.

Fears that swaps would be banned have proved unfounded to date. Central banks and regulators were concerned that so-called "off-balance-sheet products," which included swap transactions, could cause a collapse of the financial system. This systemic risk, the central banks realized, could not be controlled effectively by action taken in a single jurisdiction. If, for example, the Federal Reserve or the Bank of England banned swaps, it would probably have resulted in the movement of the transactions, and possibly the traders, offshore. So the Group of 10 countries pooled their resources and under the chairmanship of an executive from the Bank of England, established the Cooke Committee to examine ways of limiting the risks banks could take in the markets, while avoiding the problems of regulatory arbitrage.

Capital adequacy

The introduction of the first Capital Adequacy Directive was an ingenious solution to the problem. Banks were required to allocate a specific amount of capital against each transaction executed. Swaps were no longer off-balance-sheet, there was a cost of capital associated with each trade. Far from killing the market this scheme, administered under the auspices of the central bank's central bank, the Bank for International Settlements in Basle, may well have saved the swap market from an over-the-counter equivalent to Nick Leeson's exchange-traded futures and options disaster at Barings.

So in about ten years swaps had matured from an illiquid market in parallel loans to liquid markets in over-the-counter derivatives. The regulators' adroit handling of the systemic risk issues fueled the growth of the market and today many regard the major products as commoditized.

Thousands of banks and companies around the world are now regular users of the swap market. It is a liquid means by which these hedgers and traders can manage their interest rate, currency, commodity, equity, credit and climatic risks.

How Swaps Work

Overview

We have looked at the way in which swaps developed and the circumstances which encouraged their early growth. In this chapter we are going to examine the principles which govern swap transactions. Essentially there is only one type of swap and only one method for valuing swaps. A good understanding of the basic concepts provides a good foundation upon which more complex structures can be built.

Risk

A swap is essentially a way of changing risk.

> **A swap is a tool for changing risk.**

The range of risks which can be changed by entering into a swap transaction has expanded gradually over the course of the last 20 years. Currency swaps were first transacted in the late 1970s, interest rate swaps date from 1981, equity and commodity swaps from the mid-1980s and credit derivatives from 1990. Climatic derivatives are still fairly new.

Here are the major risks which can be changed with swap transactions:

- interest rate
- currency
- commodity
- equity
- credit
- climatic (weather, temperature).

This list does not contain all the possible risks which could be changed using a swap transaction, just the major markets in which swap transactions take place. Given that currency swaps in their current form, as a single legal agreement, originated in the 1970s, interest rate, commodity and equity swaps in the 1980s and credit and climatic swaps in the 1990s it is reasonable to expect other risks to be managed with the use of swap transactions. Any variable in which there are natural buyers or sellers of risk is potentially a candidate for a swap structure.

This change in risk is achieved in two stages – the two "legs" or parts of a swap transaction: the payments and the receipts. The first leg of a swap matches the existing risk, while the second leg creates an exposure to the required risk. In order to determine which way round a swap transaction needs to be structured it is necessary to look at the existing position.

> **When hedging with a swap first establish the existing position.**

The first leg of a swap transaction

Figure 2.1 shows a borrower, or an investor, and an existing position which is offset by the first leg of a swap transaction. Diagrams like this are commonly used in the swap market and are sometimes called "plumbing diagrams" or, more frequently, "boxes and arrows."

Fig 2.1

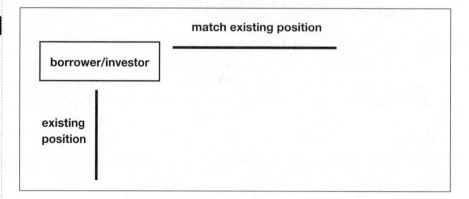

So in all interest rate swaps where the existing position is debt, the first leg of the swap is interest income which matches the interest payments of the debt.

> The first leg of a swap matches the existing position.

For example, a borrower of fixed-rate yen makes interest payments on the yen loan or bond issue and needs to be a receiver of yen interest in a swap in order to match this position. The borrower now has a cash outflow in yen: the debt; and a cash inflow in yen: the swap. The borrower has changed the company's risk. It is not possible to say, without further information, whether this is a good idea or a bad idea (see Figure 2.2).

Fig 2.2

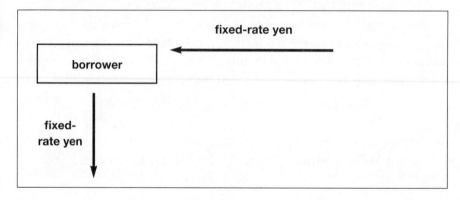

The second leg of the swap

Having matched the existing exposure with the first leg of the swap, the borrower creates the required exposure with the second leg of the swap (see Figure 2.3).

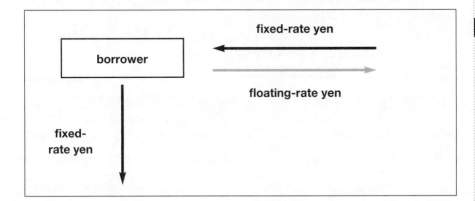

The second leg of a swap creates the required position.

Fig 2.3

An interest rate swap changes interest rate risk.

Here are some of the implications of an interest rate swap being a tool for changing interest rate risk:

- An interest rate swap is an agreement to exchange cash flows based on a given principal amount for a given time between two contractually bound counterparties.
- An interest rate swap is an arrangement which alters the interest rate basis of a cash flow.
- An interest rate swap is a method for managing debts or investments.
- An interest rate swap is a tool for asset and liability management.
- An interest rate swap changes risk.

Funding differentials, credit arbitrage, and the growth of interest rate risk management

A number of factors have contributed to the massive growth in the market for swaps. Parallel loans, back-to-back loans, the abolition of exchange controls in the UK and zero rating of the dollar premium have each contributed in part to the development of the market. International banks had a huge appetite for South American debt in the 1970s, which filled their balance sheets and increased the appeal of off-balance sheet products as swaps used to be known.

While these factors and events are important, however, the dominant driving force behind the rapid development of the swap market is the ability of different borrowers to raise funds at different rates. These funding differentials, or investor preferences, have enabled commercial and investment bankers to create opportunities for their clients to borrow at significant savings.

Credit arbitrage, first made widely known as Ricardo's Theory of Comparative Advantage fuels the swap markets.

> **An interest rate swap is an agreement to exchange cash flows based on a given amount for a given time.**

The cash flows which are exchanged in an interest rate swap can be of two types:

- specified and quantifiable flows
- specified but unquantifiable flows.

A specified and quantifiable flow could be 8% per annum, for example or US$ 800,000. A specified but unquantifiable flow could be 6-month US$ Libor. Libor is unquantifiable in the sense that it is not possible to say what the gross payments under the terms of a swap will be when the deal is struck. While Libor cannot be quantified it can be hedged, so the fact that the future rates are not known becomes irrelevant.

> **An interest rate swap is based on a notional amount.**

This is often referred to as the notional principal amount of the transaction. A typical deal might have a notional principal amount of US$ 50 million, for example. Trades tend to be for multiples of 5 million but as with other over-the-counter products the parties to the transaction are free to agree their own terms. Deals are not usually transacted on notional principal amounts which are less than US$ 1 million. Most deals would fall in a range between US$ 5 million and US$ 100 million. Much larger transactions are common.

> **An interest rate swap is transacted for a given time.**

The standard periods for interest rate swaps are one year, two years, three years, four years, five years, seven years and ten years. 30-year and 50-year transactions are not unusual.

The market in interest rate swaps has become more and more flexible and many variations are possible. In general, it is fair to say that the more unusual the transaction the more expensive the deal, or everything is possible at a price.

> **An interest rate swap is an arrangement which alters the effective interest rate basis of cash flows.**

Interest rate bases

Fixed:
- certificates of deposit
- public bond markets
- private placements
- export credits
- existing fixed-rate debt
- existing interest rate swaps
- loans

Floating:
- bank borrowings
- commercial paper
- euronote borrowings
- existing interest rate swaps
- certificates of deposit

Interest rate swaps allow users to switch from one basis to another, for example, from a fixed-rate export credit to a floating-rate bank borrowing (say 3-month Libor), or to switch within a specific interest rate type, e.g.: from 6-month Libor to 3-month Libor.

It is important to appreciate that when a hedger enters into an interest rate swap the existing debt remains in place and the borrower will continue to service the interest and principal. However, this will be offset in whole or in part by the swap transaction.

> **An interest rate swap is a method for managing debt.**

- Scenario 1: *Interest rates are expected to rise significantly.* A floating-rate borrower could consider fixing the cost of debt for whatever time horizon is deemed prudent.
- Scenario 2: *Interest rates are expected to fall significantly.* A fixed-rate borrower could consider receiving a fixed rate and paying a floating rate in a swap transaction.

> **An interest rate swap is a tool for managing assets and liabilities.**

A fixed-rate payer:

- pays a fixed interest rate in the swap transaction
- receives a floating rate of interest in the swap transaction
- has bought a swap
- is long a swap
- is called a payer
- is short the bond market
- has the price sensitivities of a longer-dated fixed-rate liability and a floating-rate asset.

A floating-rate payer:

- pays a floating interest rate in the swap transaction
- receives a fixed rate of interest in the swap transaction
- has sold a swap
- is short a swap
- is called a receiver
- is long the bond market
- has the price sensitivities of a longer-dated floating-rate liability and a fixed-rate asset.

Applications: the principal uses of swaps

- Locking in profits or unrealized gains which occur as a result of fluctuations in interest rates.

- Exploiting an advantage in one market to compensate for a weakness in another.

- Fixing the cost of debt ahead of an anticipated rise in rates.

- Matching fixed-rate assets and liabilities.

- An alternative source of new funding.

- Altering the mix of floating- and fixed-rate debt in the balance sheet.

- Potential to benefit from an anticipated fall in rates.

- Arbitraging credit differentials in the capital markets.

- Structuring products to meet investors' requirements.

The mechanics of swaps

There are three steps involved in using swaps. The first step is to identify the existing exposure. The idea in a swap transaction is to change risk and it is therefore essential to establish precisely which risk already exists. Having established the existing position, it is then possible to implement the second part of the process which is to match the existing position. All hedges are basically following the same principle, which is that the hedge creates a risk which is equal to, but opposite in direction from the existing position. This is what happens in swap transactions. The existing position is matched by a position which is equal in magnitude, but opposite in direction. Thus having eliminated the existing risk by matching or hedging it, the third part of a swap transaction creates the required risk. When a hedger wants to change one risk for another with a swap transaction, then it is done by matching the first and creating the second in the two legs of the swap.

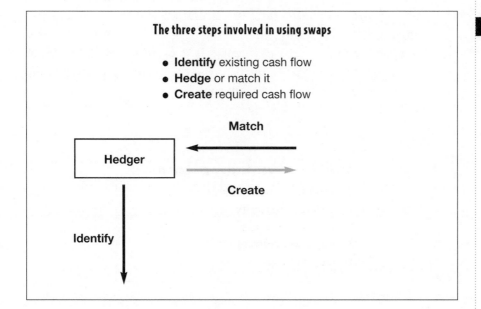

The three steps involved in using swaps

- **Identify** existing cash flow
- **Hedge** or match it
- **Create** required cash flow

Fig 2.4

Steps two and three (see Figure 2.4), matching the existing position and creating the required risk, are the swap itself. The first step, identifying the existing position, is not a part of the swap transaction, but a part of the hedging process.

Identifying existing cash flows

The hedger's objective is to create equal but opposite cash flows. In doing this the original risk will be balanced by the hedge. In order to do this effectively, it is necessary to have a very clear idea of the variables involved in the original position. Many swaps have been transacted where one of the parties to the transaction believed that they had created a hedge, only to discover subsequently that the first leg of the swap did not match the existing position. The more data the hedger has on the existing exposure the better the chance of creating a fully hedged position.

The first fundamental question is whether the existing position consists of interest payments or interest receipts. Is the structure a bullet or is there an amortization schedule? What is the principal amount? Should all of it or part of it be hedged? What is the maturity date of the underlying position? Should the swap match the maturity date, or is it designed to cover part of the period? What is the interest rate basis of the existing position? How is interest calculated? If there are reset dates for changing the interest rate, what is the basis of calculation? What is the frequency of the interest payments? Is it monthly, or quarterly or semi-annual or annual? What is the day count convention for calculating accrued interest? Are there any unusual features of the underlying position?

Investment or debt: interest paid or received

- notional principal amount
- period or maturity
- interest rate basis
- day count convention
- coupon frequency

As it is so important to determine the exact nature of the cash flow to be swapped, it is usually a good idea to write out the amounts and dates in full. These can then be compared with the flows in the swap transaction and this process will highlight matches and mismatches.

Sources of fixed- and floating-rate funds

Floating:
- Floating Rate Notes (FRNs)
- Euronotes
- Commercial Paper (CP)
- Euro CP
- Bankers Acceptances (BAs)
- Placements
- Inter-company Loans
- Certificates of Deposits (CDs)
- Interbank Deposits
- Existing Debt
- Existing Swaps

Fixed:
- Eurobonds
- Domestic Bonds
- Bank Loans
- Placements
- Inter-company Loans
- Existing Debt
- Export Credits
- Existing Interest Rate Swaps

US$ Bases:
- Libor: 1 month, 3 months, 6 months or 12 months, for example
- Prime
- CP (Commercial Paper)
- Treasury Bills (discount)
- Treasury Bonds (yield)

The principles employed to price currency and interest rate swaps are, fundamentally, those which are used to price commodity swaps, equity swaps, credit swaps and climatic swaps. They are also the principles used to price bonds, mortgages and syndicated loans. The following example shows where the boundaries of the swap market lie and how the pricing in the bond and loan market influences swap rates.

> **Swaps are an alternative financing technique, used when the cost of funds is lower than the cash market equivalent.**

Funding differentials

FOODCO/CARCORP

EXAMPLE

FoodCo is rated AAA, and requires floating-rate funds for seven years. If FoodCo were to raise money on a floating-rate basis it would cost 6-month Libor + 10 basis points. Its all-in cost of fixed-rate funds would be 7% per annum 30/360.

CarCorp is rated BBB, and requires fixed-rate funds for seven years. If it issues fixed-rate bonds then the all-in cost would be 9% per annum 30/360. Its cost of floating-rate funds is Libor + 60.

Their respective borrowing costs are as follows:

	Fixed	Floating
FoodCo	7	L + 10
CarCorp	9	L + 60

If the two companies agree to enter into an interest rate swap for seven years at 7.8% p.a. (30/360), against 6-month Libor flat, what are their respective post-swap costs of funds? Compare the cost of funds to FoodCo, through a swap, with Libor + 10, and the cost of funds to CarCorp with 9% p.a. (30/360). How much cheaper is the swap?

Fig 2.5

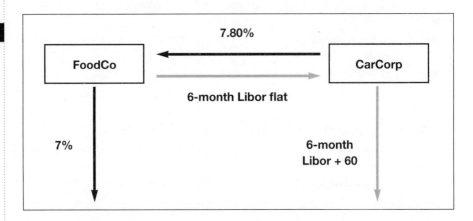

If FoodCo issues fixed-rate debt at 7% and receives 7.80% in the swap (see Figure 2.5), this generates surplus revenue of 80 basis points (0.80%) per annum. This can be used to offset floating-rate payments of 6-month Libor flat and produces a net cost of funds of approximately 6-month Libor minus 80 basis points. This is 90 basis points cheaper than the alternative for FoodCo which is to borrow on a floating-rate basis at Libor + 10 basis points.

CarCorp pays 6-month Libor + 60 for floating-rate money and receives 6-month Libor flat in the swap transaction. This results in a net cost of 60 basis points. The fixed-rate payment in the swap transaction is 7.80% so the two combined produce an all-in fixed-rate cost of about 8.40%. This is 60 basis points cheaper than issuing fixed-rate debt at 9%.

Both borrowers have benefited from this transaction. In order for this to be the case the swap rate must lie between 6.90 and 8.40. At any rate above 6.90 FoodCo will benefit from entering into a swap. At any rate below 8.40 CarCorp will benefit from the transaction. So to a large extent swap prices are influenced by the cost of fixed- and floating-rate money in the bond and loan markets.

Matching floating-rate payments: FoodCo

It is possible for the swap counterparty to net the fixed- and floating-rate cash flows so that the borrower receives a fixed-rate cash flow in the swap transaction which exactly matches the cash flow of the borrowers existing debt. The amount by which the fixed-rate cash flow is reduced is also deducted from the floating-rate cash flow in order to produce a sub-Libor cost of floating-rate money.

Swap:	7.80 p.a. bond
Amount:	US$ 100 million
Maturity:	7 years
Issue price:	100.00%
Coupon:	7.00%
Commissions and expenses:	Nil

Year	Bond issue	Swap receipt	Swap payment
0	100,000,000.00		
1	−7,000,000.00	+7,800,000	−6 m Libor
2	−7,000,000.00	+7,800,000	−6 m Libor
3	−7,000,000.00	+7,800,000	−6 m Libor
4	−7,000,000.00	+7,800,000	−6 m Libor
5	−7,000,000.00	+7,800,000	−6 m Libor
6	−7,000,000.00	+7,800,000	−6 m Libor
7	−107,000,000.00	+7,800,000	−6 m Libor
	IRR = 7.00	IRR = 7.80	

In this example if the issuer, FoodCo, made coupon payments of 7,000,000 each year against receipts of 7,800,000 from the swap transaction then it would have an annual surplus of 800,000 with which to subsidize its payments of 6-month Libor.

If however, the swap cash flow were to match the bond cash flow, what would the floating-rate payment be?

FoodCo would then receive 7,000,000 in the swap and expect to pay a sub-Libor level approximated as follows:

p.a. 30/360	s.a. 30/360	s.a. act/360
7.800	7.654	7.549
7.000	6.882	6.788
0.800	0.772	0.761

or more accurately:

(p.a. basis points * 360/((1+(1+s.a. lending rate*182.5/360))*182.5)

80*360/((1+(1+0.07654*182.5/360))*182.5)

28,800/372.08 = 77.4 basis points

So the borrower could achieve a cost of floating-rate funds at 6-month Libor minus 77 basis points or 6-month Libor – 0.77%.

Effectively each side of the transaction has been reduced by the same amount, the equivalent of 80 basis points per annum 30/360, or 77 basis points semi-annually on a money market basis.

Matching floating-rate payments: CarCorp

CarCorp borrows floating-rate money at 6-month Libor plus 60 basis points. Through an interest rate swap it switches its borrowing from a floating rate to a fixed rate by receiving 6-month Libor (flat) and paying 7.80% p.a. on a bond basis.

The total cost of CarCorp's borrowing (after netting the Libor payment and receipt) is 7.8% p.a. bond plus 0.60% s.a. money market.

If CarCorp wishes to receive Libor plus 60 basis points in the swap (in order to match its floating-rate borrowing costs), then it will need to pay the annual bond equivalent of 0.60% s.a. actual/360, plus 7.80% p.a. 30/360. We can calculate this by converting both 7.8 and 0.6 to a s.a. bond basis, adding the results and annualizing the total:

p.a. 30/360	s.a. 30/360	s.a. act/360
7.800	7.654	0.000
0.000	0.608	0.600
8.433	8.262	–0.600

Creating a par/par structure

FoodCo is the issuer of fixed-rate bonds with the following conditions:

Amount:	100,000,000.00
Maturity:	7 years
Issue price:	100.00%
Coupon:	7.00%
Fees:	2.00%

Questions

1. What are the net proceeds of the issue?

2. What is the all-in cost of fixed-rate funds to FoodCo?

3. What is FoodCo's net fixed-rate cash flow if the swap rate is 7.376% per annum?

4. What is FoodCo's cost of floating-rate funds if the swap rate is 7.80% per annum?

Answers

1. The net proceeds of the issue are 98,000,000.00. This is calculated by subtracting fees, commissions and expenses from the issue price:

$$100\% - 2\% = 98\%$$

and multiplying by the amount of the issue, 100,000,000.00.

2. The all-in cost of fixed-rate funds is 7.375985% (7.376%). This is calculated in the same way as the yield to maturity of a bond:

n is the number of compounding periods, which in this case is the same as the number of years to maturity.

PV is net proceeds of the issue. It is the amount the borrower receives and is calculated by deducting the fees, commissions and expenses from the issue price of the bond.

PMT is any cash flow which occurs with the same frequency as **n** and in this case is the coupon on the bond issue.

FV is the last cash flow and in this case is the redemption amount in the bond issue, or the amount which the borrower repays to investors.

i is the internal rate of return of the cash flow. It is the discount rate which discounts the future cash flows so that they have the same value as the first cash flow. The net present value of the cash flow is zero and the rate which achieves this is the IRR. For investors the IRR is called the "yield to maturity" and for borrowers it is called the "all-in cost."

n	i	PV	PMT	FV
7	7.376	98.00	−7.00	−100.00

3. The net cash flow (fixed) is the difference between the interest payments in the bond cash flow and the interest receipts in the swap cash flow:

Year	Bond	Swap	Net
1	−7,000,000	7,376,000	376,000
2	−7,000,000	7,376,000	376,000
3	−7,000,000	7,376,000	376,000
4	−7,000,000	7,376,000	376,000
5	−7,000,000	7,376,000	376,000
6	−7,000,000	7,376,000	376,000
7	−7,000,000	7,376,000	376,000

4. The combined present value of 376,000.00 per annum for seven years is 2,000,077.71. If the interest rate had not been rounded to 7.3760 then the answer would have been 2 million precisely.

n	i	PV	PMT	FV
7	7.376	?	376,000.00	0.00

PV = 2,000,077.71

FoodCo would therefore be able to choose between the following:

(a) Net proceeds of 98 million and swap receipts of 7,376,000 p.a.

or

(b) Net proceeds of 100 million (98 million + 2 million) and swap receipts of 7 million p.a.

Either option will neutralize FoodCo's exposure to fixed-rate debt but only (b) will fully match their fixed-rate debt.

Matching fixed-rate payments and initial cash flow

Amount:	100,000,000.00
Maturity:	7 years
Issue price:	100.00%
Coupon:	7.00%
Fees:	2.00%
Swap	7.80%

Bond	Swap: fixed	Swap: floating
98,000,000		
−7,000,000	7,800,000	− 6 m Libor
−7,000,000	7,800,000	− 6 m Libor
−7,000,000	7,800,000	− 6 m Libor
−7,000,000	7,800,000	− 6 m Libor
−7,000,000	7,800,000	− 6 m Libor
−7,000,000	7,800,000	− 6 m Libor
−107,000,000	7,800,000	− 6 m Libor
IRR 7.376	7.8	

If the swap rate was 7.3760 then the issuer could choose to receive either 7,376,000 each year and have net proceeds of 98,000,000 or it could receive 7,000,000 each year and have an initial payment of 2,000,000 (376,000 for seven years discounted at 7.3760).

If the swap rate is 7.80 the issuer could have the whole bond issue matched and pay a sub-Libor level on 100,000,000 which would be calculated as follows:

p.a. 30/360	s.a. 30/360	s.a. act/360
7.800	7.654	7.549
7.376	7.245	7.146
0.424	0.409	0.403

So the borrower's all-in cost of floating-rate funds is about 6-month Libor minus 40 basis points.

The borrower can draw down a par amount, pay 6-month Libor minus 40 basis points on the par amount and repay par. This gives borrowers the flexibility to choose par/par structures when they require them.

Swap Market Quotations and Calculations

Overview

In order to follow the detail of the swap markets it is necessary to have an appreciation of the arithmetic used in the bond markets. The swap markets bring together the ideas and conventions used in both the bond and the money markets and some of the finer points of swap pricing relate to the differences in these conventions. This chapter aims to explain these conventions and shows how they apply to swaps.

In order to follow the detail of the swap markets it is necessary to have an appreciation of the arithmetic used in the bond markets. Some of the finer points of swaps relate to the differences in the way bond and swap cash flows are treated by some market participants.

An introduction to discounted cash flow

When a bank "invests" in a company by making a loan, the investment often remains in place until the agreed repayment date.

Investors in international bonds (and other bonds) however, have an in-built flexibility to liquidate their initial investment by selling it to another investor in the secondary market. (The primary market is concerned with the issuing process itself.)

For example, if you hold bonds with three years remaining to maturity and an annual coupon (interest payment) of 7% for which you paid US$ 100.00, your cash flow would be:

EXAMPLE

	US$	
0	(100.00)	initial investment (cash out)
1	7.00	first interest payment
2	7.00	second interest payment
3	107.00	final payment (P + i)

Let us say that you bought these bonds one year ago and interest rates have now fallen by 1%. How much is your investment worth in the secondary market?

Question

We can determine this by taking the difference between the original interest rate (7% p.a.) and the current interest rate (6% p.a.) and calculating the discounted proceeds (present value) at today's interest rate of 6% p.a.

Answer

1	$1.00/1.06$	= 0.94
2	$1.00/1.06^2$	= 0.89
3	$1.00/1.06^3$	= 0.84
		$\overline{2.67}$

So we have determined that a payment of US$ 1.00 each year (US$ 7.00 – 6.00) for three years is equivalent to a once-only payment of US$ 2.67 today at a discount rate of 6% p.a.

The original investment of US$ 100.00 is therefore now worth US$ 102.67.

The new investor will buy a bond with an annual interest payment of 7% but because he is paying US$ 102.67 for every US$ 100.00 of bonds the return, or yield to maturity, is 6% p.a. The cash flows are:

	7% coupon bond	6% coupon bond
Drawdown	−102.67	−100.00
Year 1	7.00	6.00
Year 2	7.00	6.00
Year 3	107.00	106.00

Changes in bond prices reflect movements in interest rates and by adjusting for these, allow investments to be bought and sold. The change in price represents the mark-to-market value of an investment expressed in terms of today's value. The technique used to price and value cash flows in the capital markets is called "discounted cash flow." It is difficult to understand the detail of how swaps work and how the swap market functions without an understanding of discounted cash flow.

Present and future values

Discounted cash flow is a technique used widely in finance to express the value of two or more sums of money at the same date, usually so that **comparisons** can be made.

Which would you rather have, for example, US$ 100 now or US$ 110 in one year's time? There are a number of considerations in this question: what is your liquidity like – do you need money urgently? Who is offering the money? Will they be here in one year's time?

But if you are satisfied with everything else the question comes down to **which is worth more**, US$ 100 now or US$ 110 in one year's time?

In order to discount US$ 110 in one year we need a discount rate. Let's say we pick a 1-year rate of 5%.

To compound from today for a year multiply the initial amount by 1.05:

$$US\$\ 100 * 1.05 = US\$\ 105$$

Discounting is the inverse of compounding so divide the future value by 1 plus the discount rate expressed as a decimal:

$$110/1.05 = US\$\ 104.76$$

So the following statements are true, and represent calculations which are made frequently in the money, capital and derivatives markets:

$$PV * 1 + i = FV$$

$$FV/1 + i = PV$$

$$FV/PV = 1 + i$$

In each case i is the interest rate expressed as a decimal and needs to be adjusted for time.

Discount factors

A discount factor is the reciprocal of $1 + i$. If a 1-year discount rate is 5% and the amount to be discounted is 110, then there are two ways to discount the amount:

$$110/1.05 = 104.76$$

or

$$110 * 0.9524 = 104.76$$

0.9524 is a discount factor and is the reciprocal of 1.05:

$$1/1.05 = 0.9524$$

Using maturity rates

The price of a bond is the sum of the present value of its cash flows:

	Cash flow	Discount rate	Present value
Year 1	10	1.1	9.091
Year 2	110	(1.1^2)	90.909

For example, the price of a 10% coupon bond with a discount rate of 10% is par, or 100%. The return on the bond, the average annual interest received, or the yield to maturity, is also 10%. The sum of the present values of the bond's cash flows is 9.091 + 90.909, which is par, or 100%.

Calculating the dirty price given the yield

When valuing a bond on a date other than the coupon payment date it is necessary to consider accrued interest. This is a payment made to a seller of bonds to compensate for interest earned from the last coupon payment date to the settlement date of the sale.

For example, an investor sells a 10% annual coupon bond on January 16 with a 30/360 day count convention (each month has 30 days, no more, no less). The last coupon was paid on November 3.

On a 30/360 basis there are 73 days in this period so the buyer of the bonds pays accrued interest to the seller:

$$73/360 * 10\% = 2.03\%$$

What is the clean price of a 10% coupon bond maturing in 1 year 287 days (30/360) if its yield to maturity is 9%?

$$10/(1 + 0.09) \wedge 287/360 = 9.336$$
$$+$$
$$110/(1 + 0.09) \wedge 647/360 = 94.217$$
$$= 103.55\%$$

This price includes all of the next coupon, including that part payable to the seller of the bond and is known as the **full** or the **dirty price**. It is the price paid by the buyer to the seller.

In order to calculate the clean price subtract accrued interest from the dirty price:

$$103.55\% - 2.03\%$$
$$= 101.52\%$$
$$= \text{clean price of the bond}$$

Clean price = Dirty price less accrued interest.

Traders usually quote the clean price but settlement is on the dirty or full price.

Calculating yields

The yield to maturity of a bond is the average annual rate of interest earned on the cash invested. It is the discount rate which discounts the forward cash flows so that they are equal in value to the price. It is the discount rate which gives a bond a net present value of zero, so it is the internal rate of return of the cash flow:

	Cash flow	Discount rate	Present value
Year 1	10	1.1	9.091
Year 2	110	(1.1^2)	90.909

The yield to maturity on this bond is 10%, because 10% is the discount rate which calculates the price of the bond. But what is the yield to maturity if the price changes to 98.29?

In order to calculate this it is necessary to guess the discount rate, or iterate it and this process is accelerated by spreadsheets and bond calculators (see box).

Using an HP12C, 17B or 19B

The first five keys on the calculator from left to right are:

$$n \quad i \quad PV \quad PMT \quad FV$$

*(for 17B & 19Bs first find the "TVM" function from the "FIN" menu by pressing the "EXIT" key)

If you enter data in any four of these fields and press the fifth key the HP12C will calculate this "unknown."

The keys represent the following:

n = The maturity, or number of years remaining in the life of a bond
i = The yield to maturity of a bond, or return on investment assuming that the bond is held until the maturity date
PV = The price of a bond, or its present value. This is the amount paid for 100.00 units of a bond.
PMT = The annual payment on a bond, or its coupon. A cash flow which occurs n times
FV = The future value of a bond, or the amount of principal which will be repaid. This is usually 100.00% but may vary if, for example the issuer (borrower) has an option to repay the investors before the maturity date, i.e.: a callable bond ▶

So in our earlier example we would know the following:

n   = 3
i   = 6.00%
PMT = 7.00
FV   = 100.00

This data can be stored in an HP12C by pressing the following:

3 n 6 i 7 PMT 100 FV

If we next press **PV** the bond price will be calculated and displayed as

– 102.6730

The negative sign indicates that cash is being paid out, or that this cash flow is different in direction from the other cash flows.

Questions

1. Calculate the price you would need to pay for the following bonds:

Coupon	6.50%	7.75%	8.25%	9.125%
Maturity	2 years	5 years	7 years	10 years
Yield to maturity	7.10%	7.00%	9.50%	8.50%
Redemption price	100%	100%	100%	100%

2. Calculate the yield to maturity for the following bonds:

Coupon	6.25%	7.25%	8.50%	9.00%
Maturity	7 years	2 years	5 years	10 years
Price	99.50%	102.00%	97.25%	101.125%
Redemption price	100%	100%	100%	100%

Note: to input a negative number press 99.5, then **CHS**, then **PV**. On 17s and 19s use the +/– key.

Answers

Bond prices: –98.92%, –103.08%, –93.81%, –104.10%
Yields: 6.34%, 6.16%, 9.21%, 8.83%

Money, swap and bond market conventions

Monthly, quarterly, semi-annual and annual coupons

Most Eurobonds settle interest (pay a coupon) annually and the basis for calculation of interest is:

$$12*30/360 \text{ or } 30/360$$

This means that each month in a "Eurobond year" has 30 days *regardless of the real number of days in the month*.

For example – if we bought a *money market* instrument (e.g. a certificate of deposit) and held it *overnight* from February 28 to March 1, we would earn, or accrue, *one* day's interest: 28/2 –1/3 = 1 day.

If, however, we bought a eurobond for value on February 28 and held it overnight until March 1 we would accrue interest for *three* days:

> 1: February 28–9
> 2: February 29–30
> 3: February 30 to March 1

Some bonds (US treasuries, UK gilts, for example) pay interest twice each year or semi-annually. This offers the investor an opportunity to invest the interest for the first six months for the remaining period in the year, i.e. the second six months.

Let's say we compare two bonds. One pays 10% p.a. (per annum) the other 10% s.a. (semi-annually). How much interest would each pay in the first year?

$$10\% \text{ p.a.} = \text{US\$ } 10.00 \text{ for every US\$ } 100.00 \text{ invested.}$$

$$10\% \text{ s.a.} = \text{US\$ } 5.00 \text{ after 6 months and US\$ } 5.00 \text{ after 12 months.}$$

If we reinvest our first interest payment at 10% for six months (180 days) we earn 0.25%.

So our total interest is:

$$5.0 + 5.0 + 0.25 = 10.25$$

10% s.a. is therefore equivalent to 10.25% p.a. assuming a reinvestment rate of 10%.

We can perform this calculation using the compounded interest formula:

$$\{[(1 + i/n) \,^\wedge\, n] - 1\}*100$$

where:

i = the interest rate expressed as a decimal

n = the number of periods in a year, e.g. semi-annual = 2

So to calculate the annual equivalent of 10% s.a:

$$= \{[(1 + 0.10/2)\,\hat{}\,2] - 1\}*100$$
$$= \{[1.05\,\hat{}\,2] - 1\}*100$$
$$= [1.1025 - 1]*100$$
$$= 0.1025 \text{ (or } 10.25\%)$$

When converting from annual to semi-annual we perform the reverse calculation:

$$(((1 + i)\,\hat{}\,1/n) - 1) * n$$

So to convert 10.25 from annual to semi-annual:

$$= \{(1.1025\,\hat{}\,0.5) - 1\}*2$$
$$= 0.05*2$$
$$= 0.10 \text{ or } 10\% \text{ s.a.}$$

For monthly or quarterly calculations n becomes 12 or 4.

Using the HP12C to convert from s.a. to p.a. and back to s.a.

Converting an interest rate from a semi-annual to an annual basis consists of dividing the rate by 200, adding 1, and squaring the result.
For example, 10% semi-annually is equivalent to 10.25% annually:

$$(1 + (10/200))\,\hat{}\,2 = 10.25\%$$

10	÷	200	= 0.05
	+	1	= 1.05
	2	y^x	= 1.1025

Having arrived at an answer of 1.1025 it is, strictly speaking necessary to subtract 1 and multiply by 100 in order to obtain 10.25%, but the answer is clear from the result of 1.1025.

The full process for converting a semi-annual rate to its annual equivalent is as follows:

		Display
10	ENTER	10.00
200	÷	0.05
1	+	1.05
2	y^x	1.1025
1	–	0.1025
100	x	10.25

And therefore to discount an annual rate to its semi-annual equivalent involves the inverse process:

		Display
10.25	ENTER	10.25
100	÷	0.1025
1	+	1.1025
0.5	y^x	1.05
1	–	0.05
200	×	10.00

Converting from a bond basis to a money market basis

In a money market year interest is calculated as follows:

$$\frac{\text{actual number of days in period}}{360}$$

So a money market instrument held for a full, non-leap year at 10% will pay 10.1389%:

$$\frac{10*365*100}{100*360}$$

Whereas in a full eurobond year the interest calculated would be:

$$\frac{10*12*30*100}{100*360}$$

10% p.a. (money) = 10.1389 p.a. (bond)

To convert from money to bond:

$$10*365/360 = 10.1389$$

To convert from bond to money:

$$10.1389*360/365 = 10.00$$

Exercise

Starting with the following annual bond interest rates, calculate the semi-annual equivalent, the money market equivalent and the annual money market equivalent.

p.a. 30/360	s.a. 30/360	s.a. act/360	p.a. act/360	p.a. 30/360
10.25				
11.00				
10.00				
5.25				
15.30				
9.72				
7.51				

Having done this we could complete the cycle by converting the p.a. (act/360) rates to p.a. (30/360). Why do the answers differ slightly from the original numbers?

Answers

p.a. 30/360	s.a. 30/360	s.a. act/360	p.a. act/360	p.a. 30/360
10.25	10.000	9.863	10.106	10.247
11.00	10.713	10.566	10.845	10.996
10.00	9.762	9.628	9.860	9.997
5.25	5.183	5.112	5.177	5.249
15.30	14.756	14.554	15.083	15.293
9.72	9.495	9.365	9.584	9.717
7.51	7.374	7.273	7.405	7.508

The final column differs slightly because we discount from p.a. 30/360 to s.a. 30/360 at one rate and compound from s.a. act/360 to p.a. act/360 at another rate.

Exercise

If an issuer has an all-in cost of 7.376% per annum and receives net proceeds of a 7-year issue equal to 98% of the redemption value of the bond, what coupon would you suggest:

a) annually?
b) semi-annually?
c) quarterly?

As the annual coupon would be 7%, its semi-annual equivalent would suggest a coupon of about 6⅞% and the quarterly equivalent a coupon of about 6¹³⁄₁₆%.

Interest rate swap quotations

Interest rate swaps are sometimes quoted at a margin or spread above the government bond nearest in maturity to the final date of the swap. This is because the government bonds are often used as a partial hedge for mis-matched swap portfolios or books. It is of course possible to have a swap quoted in a number of different ways and familiarity with the methods of conversion from one basis to another is therefore useful in helping to give a clear understanding of the market.

5 year government yield 8.05% s.a. actual/actual

5 year swap spread 0.90% s.a. actual/actual

Swap rate = 8.95% s.a. actual/actual

What is the cost of the above swap on an annual 30/360 basis?

It is not necessary to make any adjustment for the day basis as in a full year actual/actual will generate the same amount of interest as 360/360. Dividing the semi-annual rate by 200, adding 1 and squaring the result gives 9.15%.

What is the cost of the above swap on an annual money market basis?

In this case an adjustment to the interest rate basis is necessary:

$$9.15 * 360/365 = 9.02\% \text{ p.a. (money market)}$$

Check that the two are equivalent:

$$9.15 * 360/360 = 9.15\%$$

$$9.02 * 365/360 = 9.15\%$$

If a bank quotes a 5-year swap as 90/80 then it is willing to pay governments + 80 and willing to receive governments + 90. In each case, the other side of the transaction would be 6-month Libor.

In order to illustrate that this results in the market maker earning the bid/offer spread, consider what would happen if the bank paid g + 90 and received g + 80: it would lose 10 basis points on the deals.

If you are a customer of the bank, or another bank asking for a price, you will pay g + 90 for fixed rate funds or receive g + 80 in return for a payment of floating-rate funds. This, of course, follows the principles of any bid/offer market such as futures, foreign exchange, options or commodities.

The prices of swaps indicated in the financial press or on Bridge or Reuters are intended to indicate the price at which a standard, plain vanilla or generic transaction could be executed. Factors which could influence this price include:

■ when a counterparty wants to match a swap to its own specific dates
■ when the transaction size is very large or very small
■ when there is a significant difference in the credit quality of the counterparties.

Moving swap prices

A bank calls to ask a market maker for a price in 5-year dollar interest rate swaps. The market is 80/90 but the market maker thinks rates and swap spreads are going to increase. What price should the market maker make to the other bank keeping the spread at 10 basis points?

$$81/91 \ldots \ldots 89/99$$

If for example the market maker quotes 85/95 then the bid of 85 where the market maker pays the fixed rate, is better than the market rate of 80 so if the other bank is a receiver it will deal on this price. If they are a payer they will find the quote of 95 too expensive.

$$71/81 \ldots \ldots 79/89$$

If the market maker quotes a price of 75/85, for example, then the offer of 85 is cheaper than the market price of 90, so if the counterparty is a payer, then it is likely to deal on this price.

The market maker's objective is to pay a fixed rate now in the hope of receiving at a higher level once rates and spreads have risen so it is a good idea to make the bid (pay) side of your quote more attractive than the market, that is to make it higher than 80.

If the market maker quotes 81/91 and the counterparty deals at 91 the market maker can cut out the position in the market by reversing the trade at 90 with another dealer.

The principle involved therefore is for the market maker to enhance the price on the side of the market where he wants to deal while simultaneously quoting a less attractive price than others in the market on the side where he does not want to deal.

Calculating forward/forward prices and zero coupon rates

There are three commonly used methodologies for valuing cash flows practised in the financial markets:

- using a single rate to discount the flows
- using a series of forward/forward rates
- using a series of zero coupon rates.

Single discount rates

Single rates are often used in the valuation of bonds. Fixed-rate bonds, according to ISMA's rule 803.1, should be discounted at a bond's internal rate of return, so that if an annual bond has a coupon of 5% and a yield to maturity of 5%, its price is par:

Year	Coupon	Discount	PV
1	5.00	1.05	4.76
2	5.00	1.05^2	4.54
3	105.00	1.05^3	90.70
			100.00

In this example each of the cash flows in the transaction has been discounted at the same rate. This assumes that the yield curve is flat and that it will not move. Not only are the 1-year, 2-year and 3-year rates 5%, the 1-year rate in one year's time is 5%, and the 1-year rate in two years' time is 5%.

> The compound interest formula assumes that the yield curve is flat and it will not move.

In practice this means that it is not possible to realize the values calculated by using a single discount rate. It is possible to say what a cash flow's approximate value will be, but it is not possible to lock in that value by dealing in the forward market at current rates.

Single rates are sometimes used in the pricing of floating-rate notes, although it is sometimes a rate from the short end of the yield curve which is used rather than the maturity rate used in the pricing of fixed-rate bonds. Bloomberg, for example, defaults to an assumed index which is based upon the floating-rate index mirroring the FRN's coupon frequency. If it is a floater with six monthly coupons then the assumed index will be based upon 6-month Libor. Quarterly coupons generate an assumed index which is based upon 3-month Libor.

Forward/forward rates

What if it is necessary to change these assumptions and discount a cash flow so that the calculated value is realizable. This would mean that the value calculated could actually be locked in so that it became certain. In order to do this it would be necessary to discount each of the cash flows at a forward rate. In the example above it would be necessary to discount the 3-year cash flow back to the 2-year date at the 1-year rate in two years' time.

If the 1-year rate in two years' time is 7.199% then the value of the 3-year cash flow at the 2-year date is 97.949%:

$$105\%/1.07199 = 97.949\%$$

If this cash flow is added to the existing 2-year cash flow then it produces the sum of the second and third year's cash flows, expressed at the 2-year date:

$$97.949\% + 5\% = 102.949\%$$

Repeating the process above, this cash flow can be discounted back to the 1-year date at the 1-year rate in one year's time. If the 1-year rate in one year's time is 5.051% then the value of the second and third year's cash flows at the 1-year date is 98%:

$$102.949\%/1.05051 = 98.00\%$$

Adding the first cash flow of 5% and discounting at the 1-year rate gives a present value for the whole cash flow of 100%:

$$98\% + 5\% = 103\%/1.03 = 100\%$$

So the 3-year cash flow was discounted at three rates, 7.199%, 5.051% and 3%, the 2-year cash flow was discounted at two rates, 5.051% and 3% and the 1-year cash flow was discounted at the 1-year rate of 3%. Each time the cash flows were discounted the rate used was not an assumed rate but the market forward rate for the particular period. While the answer is the same as using a single rate of 5% this is only true when a bond is trading at par.

> **When a bond is trading at par its value is the same whether calculated using the bond's yield to maturity or the appropriate forward rates.**

Once a bond's price moves away from par, then there is a difference in the valuation methods.

Calculating forward prices

In an efficient market borrowing for one year while simultaneously borrowing at the 1-year rate in one year's time should produce the same average annual cost as borrowing for two years. Using the formula employed in the money markets suggests a forward rate of 5.01%:

$$\frac{(1 + 2\text{-year rate})\,\hat{}\,2}{1 + 1\text{-year rate}}$$

$$= \frac{1.04\,\hat{}\,2}{1.03}$$

$$= 1.0501$$

$$= 5.01\%$$

But borrowing at 3% for one year and 5.01% for one year in one year's time is not equivalent to borrowing for two years at 4%:

$$1.03*1.0501 = 1.08203\% = 3.93\%\text{p.a. } (1.08203\,\hat{}\,0.5)$$

$$1.04*1.04 = 1.0816\%$$

In order to produce the break-even rate suggested by an efficient market it is necessary to calculate the forward prices by using not the curve itself, 3%, 4% and 5% but the zero coupon equivalents of these rates.

> **Calculating arbitrage free forward prices involves the use of zero coupon rates.**

Calculating zero coupon rates

If the 1-year rate is 3% per annum 30/360, then it is already expressed on a zero coupon basis. The market methodology used to calculate zero coupon rates is called bootstrapping. The name refers to the fact that a 1-year rate is used to help calculate a 2-year rate. Once this is known then 1- and 2-year rates are used to help calculate a 3-year rate, and so on. To calculate the 2-year zero coupon rate by bootstrapping we can rely on the fact that forwards, zeros and maturity rates all produce a price of par when a bond's yield and coupon are the same. This means that a 2-year bond with a coupon of 4% and a 2-year yield of 4% has a price of par when discounted at the 1- and 2-year zero coupon rates:

Cash flow	Discount rate	PV
4	3.00%	PV1
104		PV2
	Price:	100

We need to know the discount rate for the second year. or the 2-year zero coupon rate. Since we know that PV1 and PV2 add up to 100%, or par we can calculate all the components of the cash flow as follows:

$$PV1 = 4/1.03 = 3.883$$
$$PV2 = 100 - PV1$$
$$PV2 = 96.117$$

Cash flow	Discount rate	PV
4	3.00%	3.883
104		96.117
	Price:	100.000

The discount rate which discounts 104 to 96.117 can be calculated on a financial calculator as follows:

n	i	PV	PMT	FV
2	?	−96.117	0.00	104.00

So the 2-year zero coupon rate is 4.02%.

Using $FV/PV = 1 + i$ as a cross check:

$$104/96.117 = 1.08201$$

So the 2-year zero rate is 8.201% which is equivalent annually to 4.02%:

$$1.08201 \char`\^ 0.5 = 4.02\%$$

So calculating the 2-year zero rate involved taking the following steps:

- Determine a par cash flow for two years
- Discount the first year's cash flow at the 1-year zero coupon rate
- Subtract this from par
- Calculate the implied rate.

Since we now know the 2-year zero rate we can calculate the 1-year rate in one year's time:

$$\frac{1.0402 \char`\^ 2}{1.03}$$

$$= 5.05\%$$

Repeating the process for the 3-year rate, using the same steps. First determine a 3-year par cash flow:

Cash	Discount rate	PV
5.000		
5.000		
105.000		
	Price:	100.000

The first two zero coupon discount rates are known, 3% and 4.02%. Discounting the cash flows at these rates produces the following:

Cash	Discount rate	PV
5.000	3.000	4.854
5.000	4.020	4.621
105.000		
	Price:	100.000

The sum of the first two cash flows in present value terms is 9.475 and the total of the three present value cash flows is par, so the third cash flow is 90.525:

$$100 - 9.475$$

The 3-year zero rate is therefore 5.069%:

$$(105/90.525) \char`\^ 1/3$$

or

n	i	PV	PMT	FV
3	?	−90.53	0.00	105.00

Having calculated the 3-year zero rate the 1-year rate in two years' time can be calculated:

$$\frac{(1 + 3\text{-year zero rate})\,^\wedge 3}{(1 + 2\text{-year zero rate})\,^\wedge\,2}$$

$$\frac{1.05069\,^\wedge 3}{1.0402\,^\wedge 2}$$

$$1.07199$$

or 7.199%

The Users and Applications of Swaps

Overview

This chapter looks at the major institutional users of the swap markets and also at those institutions which do not themselves transact swaps but which nevertheless play a significant role in the markets. In addition to examining the types of institution active in the market it looks at what particular uses they make of swaps. What are the benefits to these organizations of being active players in the swap markets? There are detailed numerical explanations of how the transactions are structured and of the implications of different structures for the counterparties to the transactions.

This chapter starts with a summary of the major users of the swap market, outlining the uses the various institutions have for swap transactions. There is then a detailed exploration of the major uses of swaps.

The users of swaps

Governments

Governments tend to be larger users of the bond markets than the swap markets but it is not unheard of for governments to use the swap market for interest rate risk management activities, changing the proportions of fixed- and floating-rate debt in their portfolios. Most governments which run deficits fund the majority of their debt on a fixed-rate basis although some sovereign international bond issues are floating-rate notes. Many governments in Europe and beyond have used the swap market to swap fixed-rate bond issues from one currency to another or to create cheap floating-rate funds. These include

- Republic of Austria
- Kingdom of Belgium
- Canada
- Kingdom of Denmark
- Republic of Finland

- Republic of Ireland
- Republic of Italy
- Kingdom of Norway
- Kingdom of Sweden
- New Zealand.

Government agencies and municipalities

There are many government agencies, state-owned enterprises, cities and municipalities which have used the swap markets to reduce their cost of funds, or to borrow in markets where there is good appetite from investors for their bonds but where the borrower has no requirement for that currency. If, for example, the City of Bergen was offered attractively priced Canadian dollar debt, the treasurer might turn down the offer on the basis that a Norwegian city has no real demand for Canadian dollar debt. Using a currency swap, however, the attractively priced Canadian dollar debt could be swapped to produce attractively priced Norwegian krone. This means that borrowers can use the swap market to separate their funding decisions from their currency risk management decisions. Borrowing in a foreign currency creates the potential for the all-in cost of debt to be higher or lower than the interest rate as a change in the value of the currency borrowed will change the cost of funds.

> **Borrowers can use the swap market to separate their funding decisions from their currency risk management decisions.**

Government agencies and municipalities which have used the swap market include:

- Hydro Quebec
- Gaz de France
- Electricite de France
- City of Oslo
- City of Bergen
- City of Stockholm
- Japan Development Bank
- Metropolis of Tokyo
- Japan Highway
- SNCF
- Osaka Prefecture
- South Australian Government Financing.

Export credit agencies

Export credit agencies exist to provide competitively priced finance designed to boost the exports of the country in question. Export credit agencies use swaps to reduce their cost of borrowing and to diversify their sources of capital. The savings made through the credit arbitrage process can then be passed on to the local borrowers who form the client base of the export credit agencies. Some export credit agencies, especially some from the Nordic countries, have been active borrowers in the international bond markets and some have been very successful at creating funding programs which have enabled them to borrow at attractive levels. The swap market has enabled them to diversify their sources of funds, borrowing in a wide range of currencies and swapping back to the currencies of their choice. Swaps also allow these borrowers to manage their exposure to interest rate and currency risk. Export credit agencies which have used the swap markets include:

- Eksportfinans (Norway)
- Export Development Corporation (Canada)
- Swedish Export Credit
- Finnish Export Credit
- Export Import Bank of Japan.

Supranationals

Supranationals are entities which are jointly owned by more than one government. Because they have the financial backing of their governments they very often have strong balance sheets and some supranationals are considered by some institutional investors to be amongst the best credits in the capital markets. Supranational borrowers often borrow on behalf of their clients and because they are able to raise money at very attractive prices they are often able to pass on the savings to their clients. Supranationals which have used the swap market include:

- World Bank
- European Investment Bank
- Nordic Investment Bank
- European Bank for Reconstruction and Development
- Asian Development Bank
- Euratom
- Eurofima
- International Finance Corporation
- European Community
- Euratom
- Council of Europe
- European Coal and Steel Community.

Financial institutions

There is a very wide range of financial institutions which uses the swap market. It includes savings and loan associations, building societies, insurance companies, pension funds, hedge funds, central banks, savings banks, commercial banks, merchant banks, investment banks and securities houses. Hundreds of commercial and investment banks around the world are active users of swaps both for their own account and on behalf of their clients.

Banks use swaps as a trading tool, as a hedging technique and as market makers.

> **Banks use swaps for trading, hedging and market making.**

Banks can use swaps as a way of trading their view on interest rates, or their view on the way that one interest rate might change with reference to another. For example a bank could use its swap book as a way of expressing a view that the difference between 2-year rates and

5-year rates is going to increase or decrease. They can use the swap market as a tool for trading the yield curve.

> **Banks use swaps to trade the yield curve.**

Banks are also very active users of the swap market as a hedging tool. Often banks have requests from customers to borrow in maturities which it is not possible to match from a funding perspective. It is unlikely, for example, that a bank would be able to find 5-year deposits to match the 5-year fixed-rate loans made to customers. Banks can borrow in the maturities which provide the best funding opportunities and use the swap market as a way of matching their assets, or loans, to their liabilities, or deposits.

> **Banks use swaps to hedge their assets and their liabilities.**

Banks also use swaps as a way of tailoring investments to meet their clients' criteria through asset swap packages and structured products. In the same way that borrowers can use swaps to exploit their cheapest funding opportunities while having the flexibility to manage their interest rate and currency risk, investors can use swaps to change the risk on an investment to suit their requirements. If a fund manager was keen to buy a particular credit for a particular maturity in dollars but the only available opportunity was in yen then a swap would enable the investor to switch the currency risk of the investment from yen to dollars.

> **Banks use swaps as hedges to provide tailor-made investments for their clients.**

Many banks use the bond and the swap markets as a way of raising attractively priced funds for their own balance sheet. They are in a good position to spot arbitrage opportunities for themselves as they are, in any case, monitoring the markets in order to find opportunities for their clients.

Banks also use the swap market as a way of earning the bid/offer spread between the price they are willing to pay for fixed-rate money and the price at which they are willing to receive on a fixed-rate basis. This market making activity is the same in concept in every market, whether the bank is making prices in gold, spot foreign exchange, forward foreign exchange, bonds, futures, options or loans and deposits. The willingness of banks to make swap prices adds to the competitiveness of the market and helps to increase liquidity: the more banks making prices the more competitive the prices. This is true in any freely traded commodity.

> Banks add liquidity to the swap market by making markets in swaps.

Corporations

Many large companies are active users of the swap market. They use swaps for interest rate risk hedging and asset and liability matching in much the same way as banks. Some companies use the swap market to trade their view of rates and also to exploit credit arbitrage opportunities. Companies which have used the swap markets include:

- McDonalds
- IBM
- Coca Cola
- Gillette
- Shell
- ICI
- BP
- Club Méditeranée

- Intel
- Mobil
- Xerox
- Ford
- General Motors
- Walt Disney
- Philip Morris
- Pirelli

- Scandinavian Airlines
- Pepsico
- Unilever
- Eastman Kodak
- British Telecom
- Nokia
- Volvo.

There are other participants in the swap markets who don't take positions. These include various trade associations, brokers, systems vendors and publishers.

Trade associations: ISDA, IPMA, ISMA and the BBA

ISDA

The International Swaps and Derivatives Association, formerly known as the International Swap Dealers Association, is a trade association which represents the interests of the derivatives markets and the market practitioners. It grew out of a meeting of swap traders as a means of addressing the issues of non-standard documentation and central bank regulation.

> ISDA is a trade association and exists to promote the interests of swap market makers.

Every player in the market had a unique set of documentation for contracting swaps so it was a time-consuming process to negotiate the legal aspects of a swap transaction each time a bank traded with a new counterparty. ISDA's energies have in the past been focused on legal, accounting and operational issues such as standardizing documentation, netting, and the tax treatment of swaps. It acts as a lobby in the United States to promote the interests of the swap market.

IPMA

The International Primary Markets Association is concerned with the mechanics of new issues in the international bond markets. It exists to foster the interests of those issuing houses which lead manage and participate in new international bond issues.

ISMA

The International Securities Markets Association, which used to be called The Association of International Bond Dealers, concerns itself with bond sales and trading in the secondary markets.

Brokers

Brokers arrange transactions by bringing together payers and receivers. They act as intermediaries but they do not become counterparties to the transactions. In order to advertise their capacity to introduce banks to matching counterparties they often post swap prices on electronic sources such as Reuters, Bridge and Bloomberg. Once they have introduced the payer to the receiver then these two parties enter into a contract with each other. Brokers are paid a fee for their services. The major brokers in the swap market include:

- Intercapital
- Tradition
- Prebon Yamane
- Tullet & Tokyo
- Cantor Fitzgerald
- Garban/Harlows
- Cedef
- Finacor.

British Bankers Association

The BBA introduced a set of terms for interest rate swaps, known as

BBAIRS Terms (British Bankers Association Interest Rate Swap). These provide, *inter alia*, for a contract to have been struck at the time the details of the deal are agreed.

The BBA administers an essential service to the swap market in establishing a panel of banks which provide the daily quotes to calculate its London Inter-Bank Offered Rate. Rates for US dollars, Canadian dollars, Japanese yen and the euro, for example, are calculated by polling 16 banks and taking the average rate of the middle eight, thus ignoring the highest four rates and the lowest four rates.

System vendors

There is a wide array of systems available to swap market participants which facilitate the pricing of swaps and the management of deals once they become part of the bank's or the company's book. The major banks have hundreds of thousands of swaps which are revalued each day, so it is clearly necessary to have an automated process to facilitate this. Some banks develop their own internal proprietary systems, some use third party solutions, but many choose a mixture of these two approaches. It is hard to see how the market could have developed so quickly in so many currencies without the aid of information technology.

The applications of interest rate swaps

Changing a borrower's mix of fixed- and floating-rate debt

There are a number of ways in which governments, companies and banks can change the proportion of their debt on which interest is calculated on a fixed- and a floating-rate basis. Here are the three commonly used techniques which change floating-rate debt to debt which will be exposed on a fixed-rate basis:

- Pay a fixed rate and receive a floating rate in an interest rate swap.
- Buy FRAs (forward rate agreements).
- Sell three month eurodollar futures.

It would be possible to change floating-rate debt to fixed-rate debt by borrowing fixed-rate money and using the proceeds of the fixed-rate loan to repay the floating-rate debt. This technique is administratively burdensome and often very costly as there are likely to be fees charged on both loans. There are other difficulties. It may not be possible to prepay the existing floating-rate debt and it may be difficult to source fixed-rate money. Liquidity in the fixed-rate markets varies with currency, maturity, the borrower's credit quality and the economic cycle. Many borrowers therefore use swaps or FRAs or futures as a cost effective alternative.

Fig 4.1

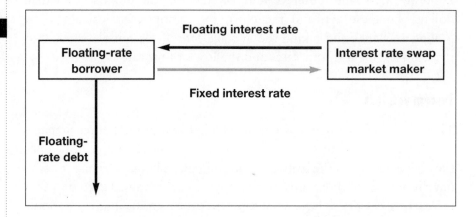

The floating-rate borrower has two exposures to a floating rate of interest. The first is the interest paid on the floating-rate debt. The second is the receipt of floating interest paid under the terms of the swap agreement.

Fig 4.2

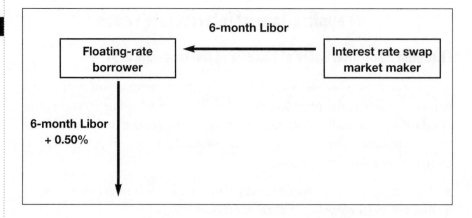

The lender of the floating-rate funds spreads the price of the loan off a floating-rate index, 6-month Libor. If the borrower pays a 50 basis point spread over this floating-rate index to the lender of the floating-rate funds then it is necessary for the borrower to receive the floating-rate index in the swap transaction in order to hedge its floating-rate risk. The floating-rate borrower's net floating-rate position is now fixed at a cost of 50 basis points. No matter what the level of Libor, the borrower is hedged from changes in the floating rate because it is both a payer and a receiver of Libor: a payer in the loan and a receiver in the swap. If 6-month Libor is 3% the borrower will pay 3.50% for the loan and receive 3% in the swap: net cost 50 basis points. If 6-month Libor is 6% the borrower will pay 6.50% for the loan and receive 6% in the swap: net cost 50 basis points.

In order to ensure that this hedge works effectively the borrower needs to tie up the mechanics of the rate setting of the loan with the rate setting of the swap. So if, for example, the Libor dates for the loan are April 25 and October 25, then the borrower needs to negotiate the same dates with the swap market maker. If Libor is set in the loan with reference to Reuters page LIBO then the borrower needs to negotiate the same rate fixing details with the interest rate swap market maker.

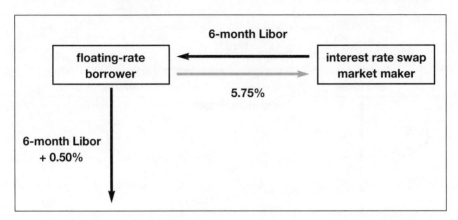

Fig 4.3

The borrower's all-in cost of funds on a fixed-rate basis is 6.25%.

$$-(\text{6-month Libor} + 50)$$
$$+\text{6-month Libor}$$
$$-5.75\%$$

Since the borrower's net cost of the two floating rates of interest is 50 basis points it is possible to calculate the all-in cost on a fixed-rate basis by adding this to the swap rate.

$$\begin{array}{r} 5.75\% \\ 0.50\% \\ \hline 6.25\% \end{array}$$

Summary

There are three commonly used hedging techniques for changing floating-rate debt to a fixed-rate basis:

- pay fixed in a swap
- buy FRAs
- sell futures.

So to change fixed-rate debt to a floating-rate basis it is necessary to enter into the reverse transactions:

- receive fixed
- sell FRAs
- buy futures.

If a borrower of fixed-rate funds has paid 5.70% and wants to change the firm's interest rate risk from fixed to floating, then receiving a fixed-rate in a swap will hedge the fixed-rate exposure and create an exposure to a floating rate of interest.

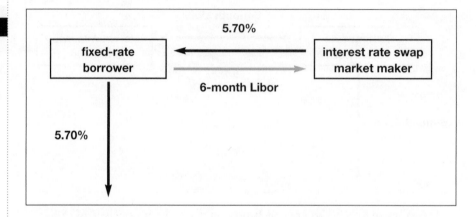

Fig 4.4

The borrower is both a payer and a receiver of fixed-rate debt at 5.70% and is a payer of floating-rate interest at 6-month Libor. The borrower's net cost of floating-rate funds is therefore 6-month Libor flat.

Credit arbitrage, reducing the cost of floating-rate money

Borrowers have created attractively priced funds through the swap markets for over 20 years. Following some USD/FRF swaps arranged as part of the financing for the Caracas metro there was a flurry of activity in many export credit related transactions. The World Bank/IBM deal in 1981 brought additional publicity to currency credit arbitrage techniques. But it was not until 1982 that the technique of issuing bonds and swapping the proceeds to reflect the borrowers required funding preference, was first combined with an interest rate swap by Banque Indosuez.

Fig 4.5

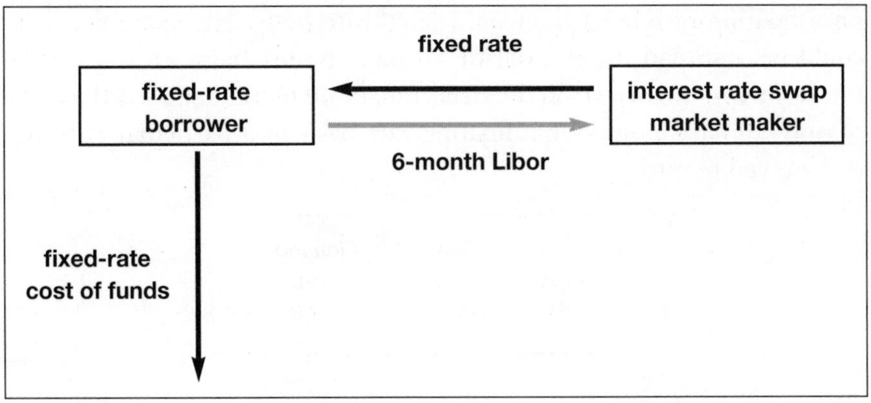

If the borrower's cost of fixed-rate debt is equal to the fixed rate paid by the swap market maker, then the borrower's all-in cost of floating-rate funds is 6-month Libor flat. If the swap rate is lower than the fixed-rate cost of funds then the all-in cost of floating-rate funds would be higher than 6-month Libor. If the swap rate is higher than the borrower's cost of fixed-rate funds then the borrower's cost of floating-rate debt is below Libor.

> **Sub-Libor funding is created by issuing fixed-rate debt at a price below the swap rate.**

The arbitrage works because of the different perspectives of the providers of funds in the bond and the loan markets. Investors who buy fixed-rate bonds, such as pension funds, insurance companies, asset managers, banks and individuals, have a different perspective on the price of credit from the banks which make loans to companies in the syndicated loan market. It is the difference between these perspectives which creates the credit arbitrage which drives the swap driven new issue process.

> **Credit arbitrage exists because there is no universal price for credit. This helps to contribute to inefficiencies in the credit markets.**

The arbitrage between bond and loan pricing has been exploited in over 40 currencies. Competition among the large commercial and investment banks to lend to the best-rated and most creditworthy corporate counterparties has contributed to very tight loan pricing. This means that there is often a tighter price differential between two credits on a floating-rate basis than on a fixed-rate basis. For example, there could be a spread differential of 50 basis points between the cost of funds for two borrowers in the fixed-rate bond market and a differential of only 30 basis points on a floating-rate basis in a particular currency and a given maturity:

	Fixed	Floating
AAA	g+50	L+20
BBB	g+100	L+50

Investor preferences, and relative investor demand for fixed-rate credits will determine the fluctuations in the spread between the cost of borrowing on a fixed-rate basis for the AAA and the BBB rated companies. In a market, for example, where credit suddenly becomes a major concern, it would be evidenced in a widening of the spread between these two particular credits. A "flight to quality" generally involves much wider credit spreads which reflect the perception that there has been a significant change in risk.

The spread differential between the cost of funds on a fixed- and a floating-rate basis can of course, be the same for two borrowers in a particular currency and a given maturity. But there is no intrinsic reason why this should be the case throughout each day of the trading year. Whenever these differentials are out of line an arbitrage arises and this window of opportunity is often exploited in the bond markets.

Fig 4.6

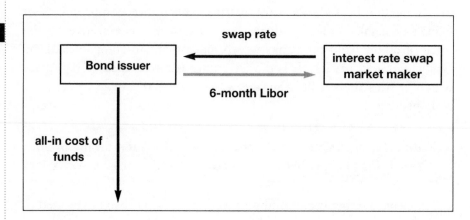

The bond issuer, or borrower, pays an all-in cost of funds for fixed-rate debt in the currency of the bond issue and swaps this exposure to a floating-rate basis. As the cost of funds is expenditure and the swap rate is revenue the cost of the floating-rate debt is determined by the difference between the revenue and the expenditure.

If the swap rate is the same as the borrower's cost of funds then the cost of the floating-rate debt is Libor flat. For example if the cost of the fixed-rate debt is 5% and the swap rate is also 5% then the cost of funds is 6-month Libor flat.

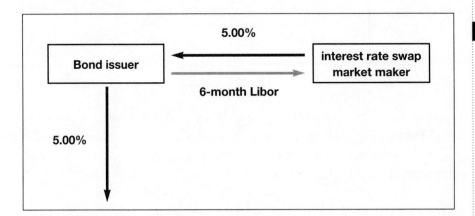

Fig 4.7

If the swap rate is higher than the cost of the original debt then the floating-rate debt is sub-Libor. For example, if the fixed-rate debt cost is 5% and the swap rate is 6% then the cost of floating-rate money is Libor less 1% or Libor minus 100 basis points.

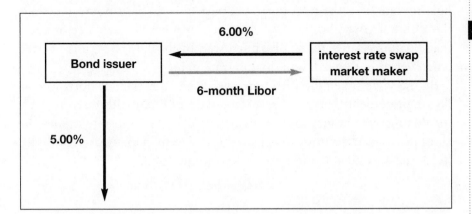

Fig 4.8

If the swap rate is less than the cost of the bond issue then the cost of the floating-rate debt is above Libor. For example if the swap rate is 4%

and the cost of the bond issue is 5% then the cost of floating-rate funds is Libor plus 1% or Libor plus 100 basis points.

Fig 4.9

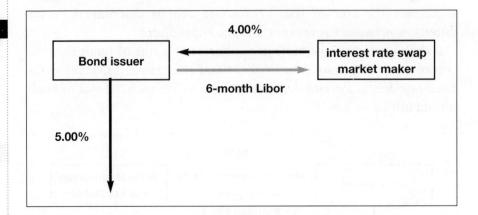

Applying these principles to our AAA and BBB rated borrowers requires looking at their natural costs of fixed- and floating-rate funds. In credit arbitrage each borrower borrows what it is *relatively* better at borrowing.

	Fixed	Floating
AAA	g+50	L+20
BBB	g+100	L+50

For the AAA issuer this means borrowing on a fixed-rate basis because it pays 50 less on a fixed-rate basis than the BBB borrower. On a floating-rate basis the AAA borrower pays only 30 basis points less than the BBB borrower. So the AAA borrower is a better borrower of fixed than floating relative to the BBB borrower. In absolute terms it is a better borrower of both fixed- and floating-rate debt.

By the same token the BBB borrower is a better relative borrower of floating-rate debt than fixed-rate debt. The BBB pays 30 over the AAA for floating-rate money and 50 over the AAA for fixed-rate money. In absolute terms it is a more expensive borrower than the AAA in both the fixed-rate and the floating-rate markets in question.

Fig 4.10

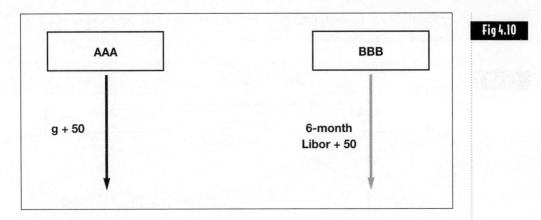

If the AAA issuer creates fixed-rate debt by launching a bond issue then it needs to receive on a fixed-rate basis in the swap transaction:

Fig 4.11

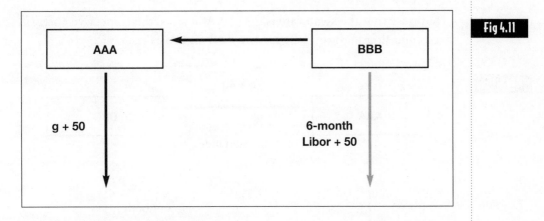

The floating-rate borrower, the BBB company, needs to receive a floating rate of interest in the swap transaction:

Fig 4.12

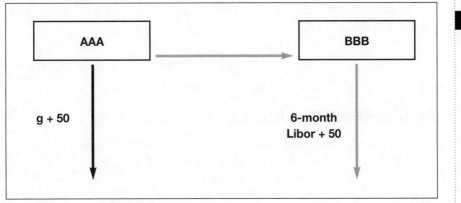

So in order to hedge their existing positions the borrowers need to construct a transaction like this:

Fig 4.13

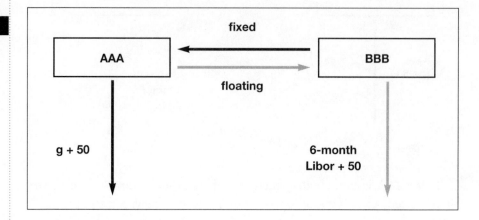

Suppose that the swap rate is g + 40. What are the respective costs of fixed- and floating-rate debt for the BBB and AAA issuers?

Fig 4.14

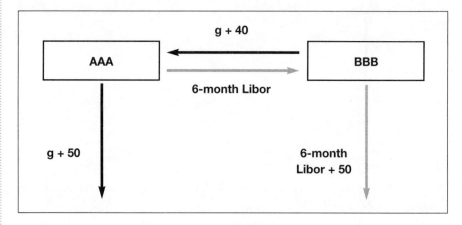

The cost of floating-rate debt to the AAA issuer is Libor + 10 basis points, calculated as follows:

$$-(g + 50)$$
$$+(g + 40)$$
$$-(6\text{-month Libor})$$

The cost of fixed-rate debt to the BBB issuer is g + 90, calculated as follows:

$$-(6\text{-month Libor} + 50)$$
$$+(6\text{-month Libor})$$
$$-(g + 40)$$

So the AAA issuer saves 10 basis points by swapping from fixed to floating by paying L+10 rather than L+20, and the BBB issuer also saves 10 basis points by paying $g + 90$ rather than $g + 100$. The combined savings are equal to the difference between the differences in their respective cost of credit on a fixed- and a floating-rate basis.

	Fixed	Floating
AAA	g+50	L+20
BBB	g+100	L+50

$$[(g + 100) - (g + 50)] - [(L + 50) - (L + 20)]$$
$$= 50 - 30$$
$$= 20$$

So the credit arbitrage is created by the different prices of credit in different markets. This happens as a result of the different motivations of institutional and retail investors in the bond markets and the competitive forces of syndicated loan pricing amongst banks in the loan markets. It can be argued that there is more efficient pricing in the bond markets than in the loan markets and that it is therefore the loans which are mis-priced. If bonds are mis-priced it is a relatively easy operation for traders to capitalize on the mis-pricing. For example, investment banks often sell short bonds which are priced very expensively and buy the underlying government bond or bond future. If the price of the credit falls (i.e., if the credit spread widens) then the trader makes money. It is therefore fairly easy to take a view on credit in the bond markets.

> **It is easier to go short of a credit in the bond markets than in the loan markets.**

Those who believe credit has been priced too cheaply in an issue can buy the credit and sell the underlying government bond or bond future. If the credit improves (i.e., if the credit spread narrows, or decreases) then the trader makes money.

> **It is usually easier to trade credit in the bond markets than the loan markets.**

It is much more difficult to trade credit in the loan markets. Loans do not, generally speaking, offer the same sort of liquidity as bonds. Many loans are totally unsuitable as trading vehicles. This deters banks from taking a view on credit and expressing it through the loan market. The development of credit derivatives has helped banks by enabling them to check the arbitrage relationship between loans and bonds and to express a view by going long (buying) or short (selling) a particular credit if their view is that it is too cheap or too expensive.

The credit arbitrage process has not altered since the early deals of the 1980s, and there are some particularly good examples of the process which do not involve a bank acting as an intermediary in the cash flow payments. This has a great advantage from a transparency perspective, as it allows the deal to be examined in detail from the viewpoint of both parties to the transaction without requiring the intermediary to disclose its profit on the transaction.

In August 1981 Salomon Bros International arranged, for an undisclosed fee, a currency swap between the International Bank for Reconstruction and Development (the World Bank) and IBM. This transaction is a particularly good example of credit arbitrage, especially as the two borrowers were both rated AAA/Aaa at the time the deal was struck. While their cost of funds in US dollars was identical there was a difference in the way Swiss investors regarded the two names and it was this view which contributed to the arbitrage possibilities which enabled the World Bank to create cheaper Swiss franc and D-mark debt than would otherwise have been possible.

The frequency of the World Bank's issuance in the euromarkets, relative to the frequency of IBM's issuance resulted in the former having to pay a premium for Swiss francs and D-marks. IBM had scarcity value among Swiss and other European investors. The fact that it was a household name and the dominant player in its industry contributed greatly to this and so it had a lower cost of funds in D-marks:

	5-year fixed-rate US$	5-year fixed-rate D-mark
IBM	16.80%	10.90%
IBRD	16.80%	11.20%
Differential	0.00%	0.30%

The World Bank could issue marks at an all-in cost of 11.20%, whereas IBM could issue marks at an all-in cost of 10.90%.

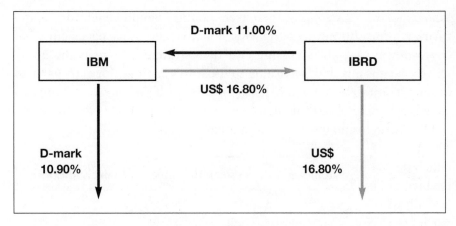

Fig 4.15

After entering into the swap the World Bank needs to net three cash flows in order to calculate its cost of funds in D-marks. IBRD pays 16.80% for its dollar debt, receives 16.8% in the swap and pays 11.0% in the swap for D-marks.

Cost of dollars from the bond issue	−16.80
Receipt from swap	16.80
Payment in swap	−11.00
	−11.00

Both the World Bank (IBRD) and IBM benefit from this transaction.

The World Bank benefits from entering into the swap transaction because it can create cheaper fixed-rate D-marks by borrowing dollars and swapping to D-marks than it could by issuing euromark bonds. This credit arbitrage exists because investors and lenders do not have a universally unanimous view of the price of credit. In other words there are inefficiencies in the credit markets of the world. The swap market enables borrowers to exploit these inefficiencies. The World Bank, and many other well rated institutions, still exploits this arbitrage today.

Credit arbitrage has its roots in Ricardo's Theory of Comparative Advantage.

Ricardo first documented this phenomenon as his Theory of Comparative Advantage in which he explained that if every country produced not what it needed, but what it could most efficiently produce and exported its surpluses, then every country would benefit. In capital market terms this means borrowing not what the issuer needs but what the issuer is best at borrowing and then swapping to what the issuer needs. So it is possible, according to Ricardo's analysis, for each party to a transaction to be a winner. This contrasts with the "no such thing as a free lunch" school of thought and also with those who say "if you don't know who's losing money in a transaction then it's you."

> **Credit arbitrage creates a link between the prices of loans and bonds.**

How asset swaps work

In its simplest form an asset swap consists of a fixed-rate bond swapped to a floating-rate basis. It is a package consisting of a bond and a swap, hence the term asset swap package.

> **An asset swap is a package containing a bond and a swap.**

An investor buys a fixed-rate bond and receives the coupon payments which are then paid to an interest rate swap market maker (fixed interest rate). In return the interest rate swap market maker pays a floating interest rate to the investor.

Fig 4.16

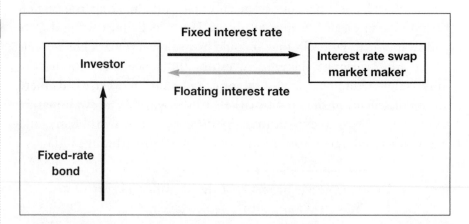

The effect of this package, a fixed-rate bond and an interest rate swap, is to provide the investor with returns which are linked to changes in the floating-rate index, often Libor, while still owning a fixed-rate bond.

Essentially the investor has a fixed-rate bond which behaves as if it was a floating-rate note.

The benefits of asset swaps

The World Bank and IBM were able to achieve a lower cost of funds than would have been possible by tapping the alternative markets directly. One of the motives issuers have for using liability swap markets is to lower their cost of funds:

> Issuers lower their funding costs with liability swaps.

Asset swaps mirror liability swaps and the motive behind them mirrors the motive for liability swaps:

> Investors enhance their returns with asset swaps.

Issuers in the eurobond market often issue in a particular currency and maturity because an arbitrage opportunity offers lower floating-rate funding. Investors in the asset swap market buy bonds because the floating-rate return is higher than that achievable in the FRN market, or the syndicated loan market. Investors may require investments which are unavailable in the floating-rate market. Asset swaps effectively reduce the supply of fixed-rate investments and increase the supply of floating-rate investments which helps to balance investor demand. Liability swaps effectively increase the supply of fixed-rate debt which helps to balance borrower demand.

> The credit arbitrage in the asset swap market enables investors to improve their return on a floating-rate basis.

Asset and liability management

The so-called "normal yield curve," or positively sloped curve, reflects, among other things, the reality that it is much easier for banks to borrow at the short end of the curve than at the long end. This means that money center banks can fund themselves much more effectively in the interbank market in maturities such as the overnight, tom/next (overnight from tomorrow, or tomorrow to the next day), spot/next, one week, one month, three months and six months than they can in maturities such as five years or 20 years.

What if a bank has substantial demand for fixed-rate funds from its customers in longer-dated maturities? There are a number of possibilities. Launching a bond issue may be an appropriate solution. Encouraging the customer to consider floating-rate funding is another. In either of these cases the bank would have matched assets (loans to customers) and liabilities (funding).

Another option open to the bank is to borrow at the short end of the curve on a floating-rate basis and lend at the longer end of the curve on a fixed-rate basis. This technique is called "borrowing short and lending long," and many bankers over many years have been given the advice "don't borrow short and lend long."

It seems like a particularly attractive idea when there is steep slope in the curve. Say for example that 3-month money costs 5% in the interbank market and that the 5-year government rate is 8%. A bank could perhaps make a 5-year fixed-rate loan to a customer at 9%, adding a credit spread of 1% to the government curve, and fund the loan at 3-month Libor of 5%. If the bank has a view that interest rates are likely to fall, remain as they are, or increase slightly then this can seem like a very attractive business opportunity. Many banks over the years have found it too tempting to turn down and some have suffered large losses as the cost of the funding rises with an upward move in rates.

With the development of the swaps market it is possible for banks to satisfy their customers' demands for fixed-rate funding while ensuring that the bank's assets and liabilities are matched.

Suppose a bank has a customer who needs 5-year fixed-rate funds. Let us say that the bank finances this loan in the interbank market at 3-month Libor. The bank now has a 3-month liability and a 5-year asset (see Figure 4.17). The bank is short floating-rate interest at 3-month Libor and long fixed-rate interest at the rate at which it lends to its customer. This is the asset and liability mismatch discussed above. So in order to hedge its position the bank needs to match its exposure to 3-month Libor by receiving on a floating-rate basis in an interest rate swap, and match its exposure on a fixed-rate basis by paying a fixed-rate in an interest rate swap. This is a hedge which is ideally suited to an interest rate swap in which the bank receives a floating rate of interest and pays a fixed rate (see Figure 4.18).

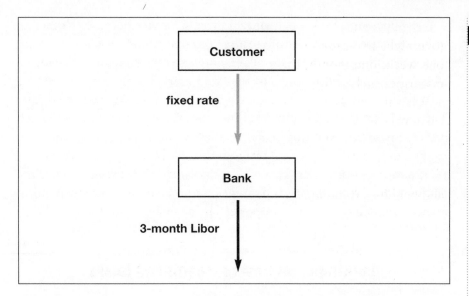

Fig 4.17

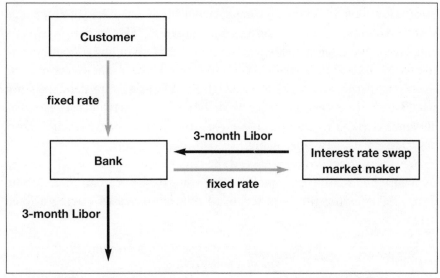

Fig 4.18

This structure has the benefit for the bank that it eliminates the banks exposure to interest rate risk. The bank can no longer profit from a fall in interest rates but it cannot lose money on its asset and liability mismatch as a result of an increase in rates. The bank will make or lose money based on its pricing of the credit risk in the transaction and its overall loan exposure rather than on its ability to forecast interest rates. So the bank is in the credit business not the trading business.

Interest rate swaps provide banks with an opportunity to change their risks from interest rate to credit.

Banks' customers also benefit from this structure because the facility to borrow at fixed rates of interest is not conditional on finding a bank which is willing to punt (speculate) interest rate risk on behalf of its clients. Any bank with access to the swap markets can create fixed-rate debt by borrowing on a floating-rate basis and swapping to a fixed rate. The fixed rate in the swap market becomes the benchmark from which banks can price fixed-rate loans to their customers. This means that banks can be active lenders of term funds for two years, three years, five years and even out to ten years. Corporate and retail customers have the flexibility to choose fixed- or floating-rate funds based on their requirements rather than on what happens to be available from their bankers.

Locking in interest rate gains and losses

Suppose a borrower has floating-rate debt and has decided to change this to fixed-rate debt as a result of a change in the company's interest rate risk management strategy. One method of changing a floating-rate loan to a fixed-rate loan is to borrow fixed-rate money and use the proceeds of this new debt to repay the old floating-rate debt. It is not usually a very popular choice with borrowers partly because of the shortage of fixed-rate money but mostly because of the transaction costs associated with new borrowing.

An alternative strategy would be to hedge the floating interest exposure by creating an equal but opposite position in an interest rate swap and creating the required fixed-rate exposure by paying a fixed rate in the swap.

Fig 4.19

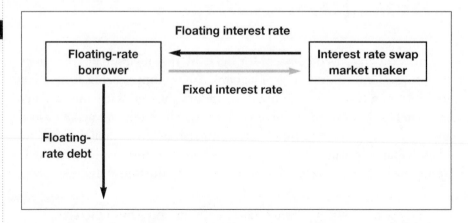

This technique can also be used to change fixed-rate debt to floating-rate debt. The same arguments apply. The borrower could change the exposure by borrowing new money on a floating-rate basis and using the drawdown proceeds to repay the existing fixed-rate debt. Prepayment penalties could be a deterrent, or if the fixed-rate debt is an outstanding bond issue it may be impossible to find all the bonds. But once again the transaction costs are the most likely deterrent to this approach.

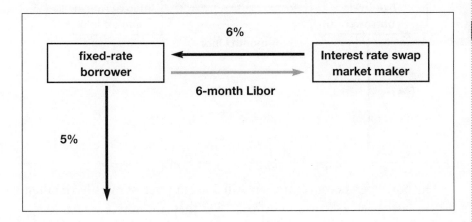

Fig 4.20

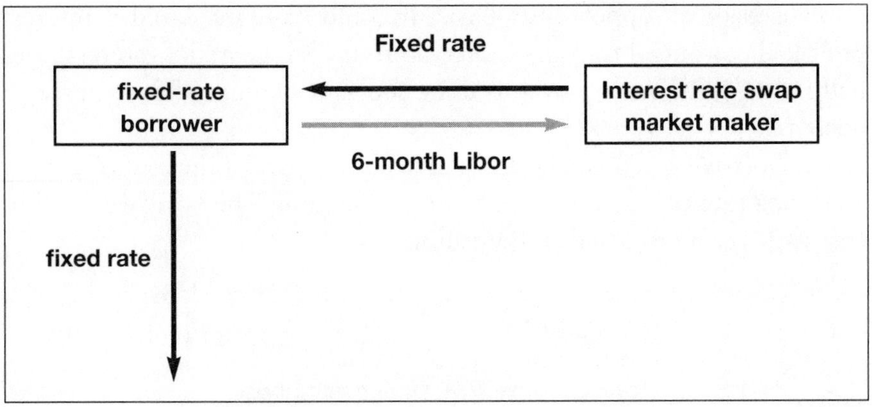

Locking in interest rate gains

An alternative technique would involve the payment of a floating rate of interest in a swap and the receipt of a fixed rate.

If the swap rate is at the same price as the existing fixed-rate debt then the floating exposure is created at Libor flat.

If the swap rate is above the price of the existing fixed-rate debt then the floating exposure is created at a sub-Libor level.

Fig 4.21

In the example in Figure 4.21, the borrower has an exposure to existing debt at 5% which represents expenditure. In the interest rate swap the borrower is paid a fixed rate of 6%. This is revenue. So the net of the borrower's expenditure and revenue is a gain of 1%:

$$+6\%-5\% = +1\%$$

The borrower has therefore locked in a gain of 1% by entering into the swap transaction. Before executing the swap the gain was on an unrealized or an opportunity basis. It could have increased if interest rates had continued to rise, or decreased or disappeared if interest rates had fallen. But now the swap is done the gain cannot either increase or decrease.

The borrower can use the 1% gain to offset part of the cost of paying a floating rate of interest in the swap transaction. The borrower's all-in cost is therefore 6-month Libor minus 1%.

Funding cost	−5.00%
Fixed receipt	6.00%
Floating payment	− 6-month Libor
All in cost	− (6-month Libor −1%)

Locking in interest rate losses

If the swap rate is below the price of the existing fixed-rate debt then the floating exposure is created at a level above Libor:

Fig 4.22

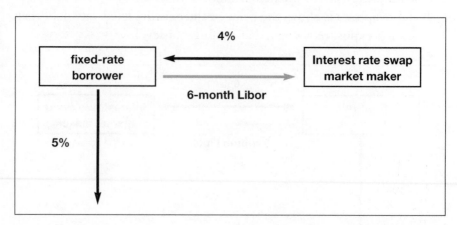

The borrower's cost of funds is still 5% but interest rates have fallen. If the borrower executes a swap at 4% then the interest rate loss is locked in. Prior to the execution of the swap, the borrower's loss could increase or decrease, but after its execution, it is fixed at a loss of 1%. The borrower's all-in cost of funds is therefore 6-month Libor plus 1%.

Funding cost	–5.00%
Fixed receipt	4.00%
Floating payment	– 6-month Libor
All in cost	– 6-month Libor +1%

In the cases above the borrower is locking in interest gains or losses. Prior to the swap transaction the mark to market gains or losses on the borrower's fixed-rate debt are opportunity gains or losses and as such could become greater or smaller. Once the swaps are transacted the gains or losses become realized.

The swap is the tool for taking the gain or loss. It does not create it.

Changing an investor's portfolio mix of fixed- and floating-rate investments

It is possible to change the revenue stream of an investor's fixed-rate bond by swapping the cash flows to a floating-rate basis. This transaction is often called an asset swap.

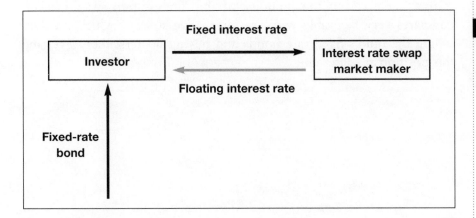

Fig 4.23

It is also possible for a portfolio manager to hedge the whole or part of a portfolio using interest rate swaps. If a fund manager takes a view that interest rates are likely to rise over a given period, say two years, it may not be appropriate to sell fixed-rate bonds and buy floating-rate notes. There are potential capital gains and losses to be taken into consideration and the bid/offer spread in the bonds if the position is reversed at a later date.

An interest rate swap allows the portfolio manager to reduce the fund's exposure to fixed rates of interest by hedging the fixed-rate revenue of the fund and creating floating-rate revenue. The fund therefore receives floating and pays fixed in an interest rate swap. This is the same structure as an asset swap.

Fig 4.24

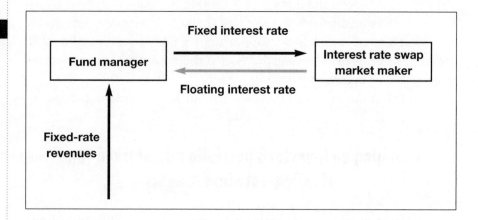

This transaction can be terminated during its life if the fund needs to change its view. It is therefore a very flexible solution and the cost of transacting it, given the liquidity of the interest rate swap market, compares very favorably with the alternative strategy which involves selling the fund's fixed-rate bonds and buying floaters, then reversing this position at a later date.

Market Making, Trading and Structuring Swaps

Overview

This chapter discusses the motives of banks for the warehousing of swaps, before examining the impact of the Capital Adequacy Directive on the development of swaps – in particular the growth of the basis swaps market as a result of the relative penal treatment of currency swaps over interest rate swaps from a capital adequacy perspective. It shows how swaps developed as a tool for the management of multi-currency debt portfolios and how swaps are used as a method of diversifying the sources of funds for international borrowers. The credit arbitrage process is examined in detail and there are exercises which illustrate the calculation of a bond issuer's fixed-rate cost of funds and its post-swap cost of floating-rate funds. The relationships between annual and semi-annual basis points and between money market and bond market day-count conventions are illustrated in the case studies.

Introduction

The original participants in the swaps market arranged their transactions so that there were no open positions. If a client had an interest to pay fixed-rate Norwegian kroner and receive fixed-rate D-marks, for example, then the bank would search for a counterparty with an opposite interest. While the search was in progress the original client would still have exposure to the risks it was attempting to hedge. Suppose that the client had D-mark debt and wanted to reduce its exposure to the D-mark and increase its exposure to the kroner. The client would be exposed to an appreciation of the D-mark against the kroner while its banks searched for a counterparty.

While this represented a clear disadvantage for clients, there were weaknesses in this system for banks. Although banks had no exposure to currency or interest rate risk as a result of their client's request to transact a swap the bank ran the risk that a competitor would find a match first. The system was also inflexible in that it was not only necessary to find two parties with opposite exposures, but also a requirement that the maturities and amounts the parties wanted to hedge were identical.

It was not long before banks decided that in order to compete more effectively with each other and offer a more useful service to their clients they would offer instant execution and warehouse positions in the market. In 1982 Citibank became the first bank to take a position in the swap market, hedging its exposure in the Treasury Bond futures market.

Market making in swaps soon followed as the growth of both exchange-traded interest rate futures and over-the-counter forward rate agreements contributed to greater liquidity and helped to fuel demand for interest rate risk hedging products. Membership of the International Swap Dealers Association grew from ten houses at its inception in 1985 to almost 50 houses one year later.

The close relationship between FRAs, futures and swaps and between foreign exchange forwards and currency swaps provided banks with an opportunity to sell treasury solutions to their customers in a way that would have been hard to imagine five years earlier. Not only was it possible for banks to provide their customers with effective interest rate and currency management tools, it was also possible for a much wider range of banks around the world to offer these solutions to an increasingly large number of corporate and institutional clients.

The first capital adequacy directive in 1988 had a major impact on banks' trading activities in the swap markets. Prior to the Basle Accord, banks often took positions in the currency swap market in order to win customer business. Often these positions involved currency and interest rate risk and banks were understandably keen to close out the risks quite quickly. Currency volatility, in particular, could quickly turn a good trading month into a poor one.

But the capital adequacy rules formulated by the world's leading central banks and coordinated by the Bank for International Settlements in Basle recognized the greater risks faced in the currency swap market by banks than those they faced in the interest rate swap market and the rules sought to encourage banks to reduce their currency exposure or set aside considerably more capital for them than they might for an interest rate swap. This had quite a dramatic effect on market participants. Prior to the accord most currency swaps were quoted against 6-month US$ Libor so there was a common unit in all currency markets.

If a customer wanted to hedge yen debt while simultaneously creating a sterling exposure it would be possible for their bank counterparty to hedge this position with two swaps against 6-month US$ Libor. In the first swap the customer receives fixed-rate yen and pays 6-month US$ Libor. In the second swap the customer receives 6-month US$ Libor and pays a fixed rate of interest in sterling. Both of these transactions count as currency swaps for capital adequacy purposes.

But the Basle Accord made this a very expensive operation from a capital adequacy perspective. A relatively straightforward 2-year currency swap could consume up to five times as much capital as an interest rate swap for the same maturity. Banks had, for the first time, a powerful incentive to structure transactions as interest rate swaps wherever possible.

This phenomenon gave rise to the birth of the currency basis swap market. Under this structure a customer hedging yen debt by increasing its exposure to sterling might have its position hedged not with two currency swaps but with two interest rate swaps and a cross-currency basis swap. In the first interest rate swap the hedging bank would receive a fixed rate of interest in yen and pay a floating rate of interest in yen. In the second interest rate swap the hedging bank would pay a fixed rate of sterling interest and receive a floating rate of sterling interest. In the cross currency basis swap the hedging bank would pay a floating rate of sterling interest and receive a floating rate of yen interest.

While the structure appears to be more complicated it has the big attraction of enabling more interest rate swap transactions to be executed and reducing the number of currency swap transactions. This has the effect of reducing the amount of capital banks require to support their swap activities.

The growth of the basis swap market gave an enormous boost to the interest rate swap markets around the world. Rather than currency swaps remaining the preserve of a relatively small number of international banks they now became a domestic trading instrument suitable for any bank with interest rate risk positions. This provided much greater liquidity than would have been likely under the earlier regime.

Before capital adequacy was imposed upon the markets some bank traders had believed that swaps were unlikely to last as a product. Regulators could have banned them from their jurisdiction which might have resulted in the swap markets being driven offshore. Capital adequacy had a tremendously reassuring effect on traders as it became increasingly clear that the concern of the regulators was not the risk of one institution defaulting on its payments but the effects this might have on the banking system. One regulator said, off the record, that if a bank was determined to go out of business there was not much the central bank could do about it. The central bank's function, he said, was to ensure that the banking system was not threatened.

So traders could now relax, secure in the knowledge that their central banks were keen for them to manage their returns on capital. Trading in swaps was limited now not by the size of a firm's interbank swap credit lines but by the amount of capital the firm was willing to allocate to its swaps traders.

An unhedged swap transaction with no other transactions attached to it provides an opportunity to take a view on interest rates. A payer of a fixed rate hopes that interest rates will rise and will be rewarded with a profit if they do and a loss if they don't. Swaps aren't necessarily the most efficient way to take this view. Where interest rate futures contracts exist there is often a cheaper means to achieve the same end. But banks which are active market makers in the swaps market daily find themselves with positions which can either be hedged or traded.

Uses of currency swaps

Altering a borrower's mix of currency debt

In the same way that it is possible to use an interest rate swap as a means of changing the proportions of fixed- and floating-rate debt in a borrower's portfolio it is possible to use a currency swap as a means of changing the proportion of currency debt in a multi-currency debt portfolio. Suppose a company has borrowed half its debt in US dollars and the other half in Swiss francs. The currency debt management committee has reviewed the company's currency activities and has decided that the firm should reduce its exposure to the dollar and increase its exposure to the franc.

One way of achieving this would be for the company to borrow Swiss francs, sell the proceeds of the borrowing spot, and buy US dollars. The dollars could be used to prepay some of the existing dollar debt, thus reducing the firm's exposure to the dollar and increasing its exposure to the franc.

While this strategy complies with the decision of the currency risk management committee it could be difficult and expensive to achieve it, because of the transaction costs associated with drawing down new debt and prepaying existing debt.

A cheaper alternative would involve the firm in receiving a fixed rate of interest in US dollars and paying a fixed rate in Swiss francs.

Fig 5.1

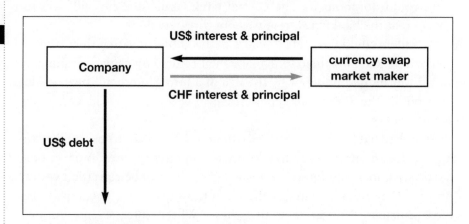

This has the same outcome as the strategy above in that the firm reduces its exposure to the dollar and increases its exposure to the franc, but it is likely to be achieved at a fraction of the cost. Since this is so it makes the currency swap a very flexible tool in the management of multi-currency debt portfolios. Whenever a firm needs to alter the mix of currencies in its portfolio it can receive interest on those where it needs to reduce its exposure and pay interest on those where it needs to increase its exposure.

Diversifying a borrower's source of funds

Traditionally companies and institutions borrow money in those markets where there is adequate supply of funds, or a sufficient appetite for their credit, and in maturities and currencies which fit the borrower's overall funding strategy.

The ability to hedge medium- and long-term currency exposures means that companies can raise money in those markets where there is demand for their name regardless of whether the currency fits their strategy. For example, let's say that a German bank has no business in Australia and therefore no requirement for Australian dollar debt. On the contrary the bank might well be very keen to ensure that there are no currency mismatches in its debt portfolio.

The bank could, however, be well enough known among investors in Australian dollar bonds to make demand for its paper sufficiently high to offer it a competitive cost of funds in Australian dollars. The currency swap market enables the bank to capitalize on this opportunity by borrowing Australian dollars, receiving Australian dollars in a currency swap and paying the currency of its choice, say floating-rate US dollars:

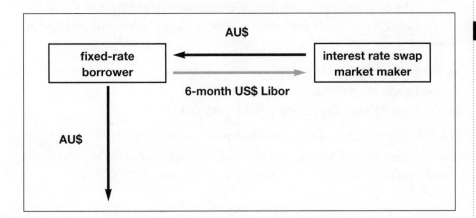

Fig 5.2

This means that borrowers can borrow wherever there is demand for their credit, not simply in those markets where the currency fits their exposure management objectives. Funding and currency risk management therefore become separate functions within the firm.

Credit arbitrage, reducing the cost of floating-rate money

The cost of funds to a borrower in one market may well be the same as it is in another when the funding costs are compared to a government benchmark, for example. Suppose a borrower pays 30 basis points more than the Japanese government for 5-year yen debt. Is it reasonable to assume that the same borrower will pay 30 basis points more than the US Treasury for US dollar debt? Often this will be the case, but it is possible that different supply and demand considerations in the yen and US dollar markets could result in a difference.

Borrowers and their banking advisors therefore routinely compare the cost of floating-rate money created in one market with the cost of the same floating-rate index created in another. For example, if a borrower issues fixed-rate yen debt and swaps to floating-rate US dollars, does this result in cheaper money than issuing fixed-rate D-mark debt and swapping it to floating-rate US dollars?

A borrower issuing fixed-rate debt in one currency and entering into an interest rate swap effectively changes the nature of the debt from fixed to floating. This is the effect of the hedge rather than a reflection of the reality as the borrower still has fixed-rate debt. It is because the swap hedges the borrower's exposure to fixed-rate debt while simultaneously creating an exposure to floating-rate debt that it is said that the borrower's risk has changed.

In order to quantify this change it is necessary to examine in detail the three cash flows which represent the borrower's exposure to interest rate risk:

- the cost of fixed-rate money
- the fixed-rate revenue received in the swap
- the floating-rate expenditure paid in the swap.

The borrower essentially has two lots of expenditure and one of revenue and the post-swap all-in cost of floating-rate debt is the net cost of these three items.

Calculating the all-in cost of funds on a fixed-rate basis

The fees and expenses in a bond issue are paid by the borrower, usually as a deduction from the proceeds of the issue. So the net proceeds of an issue are the funds paid by the lead manager to the borrower on the payment date, or the date from which interest accrues. Let's look at an example of a bond issue and calculate the issuer's all-in cost of funds.

Amount	NOK 400,000,000
Maturity	Six years
Coupon	7% per annum
Issue price	101.65%
Amortization	Bullet
Call option	If taxation changes
Listing	London Stock Exchange
Commissions	1⅞%: selling 1¼%,
	management and underwriting ⅝%
Governing law	English
Negative pledge	None
Cross default	Yes
Force majeure	Usual provisions
Pari passu	Yes
Launch date	November 21
Payment date	January 15
Swap	7.15% per annum (30/360)
Market sector	Eurobond
League table	Yes

In order to calculate the borrower's cost of fixed-rate Norwegian krone it is necessary to establish the cash flows which result from their decision to issue fixed-rate bonds. With a coupon of 7% and redemption at par the forward flows are as follows:

1	–28,000,000	(7/100*400,000,000)
2	–28,000,000	(7/100*400,000,000)
3	–28,000,000	(7/100*400,000,000)
4	–28,000,000	(7/100*400,000,000)
5	–28,000,000	(7/100*400,000,000)
6	–28,000,000	(7/100*400,000,000)
6	–400,000,000	(100/100*400,000,000)

The borrower's net proceeds are calculated by deducting the commissions from the issue price:

Issue price	101.650%
less commissions	1.875%
Net proceeds	99.775%

So the net proceeds are NOK 399,100,000 which is 99.775% of NOK 400 million, and the borrower's complete cash flow looks like this:

0	399,100,000.00	(99.775/100*400,000,000)
1	−28,000,000.00	(7/100*400,000,000)
2	−28,000,000.00	(7/100*400,000,000)
3	−28,000,000.00	(7/100*400,000,000)
4	−28,000,000.00	(7/100*400,000,000)
5	−28,000,000.00	(7/100*400,000,000)
6	−28,000,000.00	(7/100*400,000,000)
6	−400,000,000.00	(100/100*400,000,000)

The borrower's all-in cost of funds is the interest rate which discounts the forward cash flows to NOK 399,100,000 and can be calculated as follows:

n	i	PV	PMT	FV
6		399,100,000.00	−28,000,000.00	−400,000,000.00

The borrower's all-in cost of funds is therefore 7.047% per annum (30/360).

The swap counterparty is willing to pay 7.15% per annum on a 30/360 day count basis in return for 6-month NOK Libor (flat).

Fig 5.3

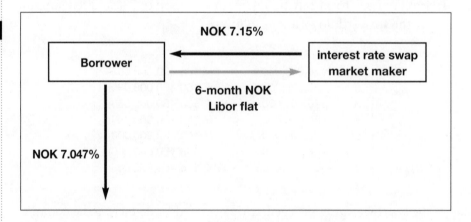

Calculating the all-in cost of funds on a floating-rate basis

After transacting the swap as illustrated above the issuer would have the following fixed-rate cash flows.

	Bond issue	Swap
0	399,100,000.00	
1	−28,000,000.00	28,600,000.00
2	−28,000,000.00	28,600,000.00
3	−28,000,000.00	28,600,000.00
4	−28,000,000.00	28,600,000.00
5	−28,000,000.00	28,600,000.00
6	−28,000,000.00	28,600,000.00
6	−400,000,000.00	

The borrower has agreed to pay 6-month Norwegian krone Libor on 400 million krone, and will repay the bondholders 400 million krone. As a result of the commissions paid to the management group the issuer will receive 399.1 million krone. Subject to negotiation with the swap counterparty it is possible for the issuer to create a "par/par" structure by giving up their entitlement to some of the annual fixed-rate swap payments in return for an initial payment of 900,000 krone. The swap counterparty might, for example, agree to make this payment in return for reducing the annual swap payment from 28,600,000 krone to 28,410,000 krone.

0	399,100,000.00	900,000.00
1	−28,000,000.00	28,410,000.00
2	−28,000,000.00	28,410,000.00
3	−28,000,000.00	28,410,000.00
4	−28,000,000.00	28,410,000.00
5	−28,000,000.00	28,410,000.00
6	−28,000,000.00	28,410,000.00
6	−400,000,000.00	

Having agreed the above, the issuer's fixed-rate cash flow now looks like this:

	Net fixed-rate cash flow
0	400,000,000.00
1	410,000.00
2	410,000.00
3	410,000.00
4	410,000.00
5	410,000.00
6	410,000.00
6	−400,000,000.00

It is usual market practice to use the mismatched fixed-rate amount, NOK 410,000 per annum, to subsidize the floating cash flows. NOK 410,000 is approximately equal to 6-month Libor minus 10 basis points.

Calculating a borrower's all-in cost of funds

Amount	100 million
Maturity	Four years
Coupon	7.5% per annum
Issue price	101
Amortization	Bullet
Call option	If taxation changes
Listing	London Stock Exchange
Commissions	1⅜%: selling ⅞%, management and underwriting ½%
Governing law	English
Negative pledge	None
Cross default	Yes
Force majeure	Usual provisions
Pari passu	Yes
Launch date	November 21
Expenses	50,000.00
Swap	7.80% per annum (30/360)
Market sector	Eurobond
League table	Yes

The cash flows resulting from the bond issue result in an all-in cost of 7.552% for the issuer:

Net proceeds	99,825,000.00
Year 1	−7,500,000.00
Year 2	−7,500,000.00
Year 3	−7,500,000.00
Year 4	−7,500,000.00
Year 4	−100,000,000.00

This is the discount rate which discounts all the forward cash flows in years one, two, three and four to a present value of −99,825,000. When this amount is deducted from the net proceeds the result is zero and when the net present value of a cash flow is zero the discount rate is said to be the internal rate of return (IRR). The convention in the international bond markets is to reflect the borrower's average annual cost of funds as an internal rate of return and it is referred to as "the borrower's all-in cost."

The issuer's cash flows resulting from the swap are:

Year 1	7,800,000.00
Year 2	7,800,000.00
Year 3	7,800,000.00
Year 4	7,800,000.00

So the borrower needs a cash flow with a value of 7.552% in order to match its all-in cost of fixed-rate debt. The surplus, that is the extent to which the swap rate is higher than the borrower's cost of funds, creates the sub-Libor level. Adjusting for the difference between an annual bond (30/360) basis and a semi-annual money market basis reduces this to approximately 24 basis points, calculated as follows.

Discounting 24.8 basis points per annum (7.80%, the swap rate, less 7.552%, the borrower's cost of funds) over four years at 7.80% produces a present value of 82.51 basis points.

n	i	PV	PMT	FV
4	7.8	−82.51	24.80	0.00

This is 12.17 basis points expressed semi-annually on an 30/360 basis, compounded to a semi-annual rate at 7.654%, the semi-annual equivalent of 7.80%:

n	i	PV	PMT	FV
8	7.654/2	82.51		0.00

12.17 on a 30/360 basis is equivalent to 12.0 on an actual/360 basis:

$$12.17*360/365$$

So 12 basis points in two semi-annual periods (actual/360) is equivalent to 24.8 basis points per annum (30/360). It is necessary to double this to 24 basis points to express it as a sub-Libor level as 6-month Libor is expressed as approximately double the amount paid in each semi-annual period. Therefore 24.8 basis points per annum on a 30/360 basis is equivalent to 24 basis points semi-annually.

Reversing the process we can calculate the annual bond equivalent to 6-month Libor minus 24 basis points:

$$(1 + (0.24\% * 182.5/360))(1 + (0.24\% * 182.5/360))$$

This gives an answer of 24.3 basis points and reflects the fact that the semi-annual rate has been compounded at 0.24% semi-annually. The compound interest formula compounds and discounts at the original rate and in practice this would result in the swap counterparty making a series of small loans to the issuer at 0.24%. If the swap counterparty wants to charge the market price for the loans it is necessary to compound the semi-annual basis points at a market rate. If the rate for the loans is 7.80% per annum or 7.654 semi-annually the calculation becomes as follows:

$$[(24 * 182.5/360)((1 + (0.07654 * 182.5/360))] + 24 * 182.5/360$$
$$= 24.81 \text{ basis points per annum}$$

Now the swap counterparty is lending the money at the swap rate rather than at 0.24%.

The swap market maker receives a lower payment at the end of each six monthly period as the borrower pays Libor minus 24 rather than Libor flat. The swap counterparty is able to recoup the proceeds of these loans by lowering the annual swap payment, in this transaction from 5.80% per annum (30/360) to 5.552% per annum. So for the second six months of each year the swap market maker makes a loan to the borrower which is repaid at the following annual coupon payment date.

To convert semi-annual (actual/360) basis points to their annual equivalent:

$$[(s.a. \text{ basis points} * 182.5/360)((1 + (s.a. \text{ lending rate} * 182.5/360))]$$
$$+ s.a. \text{ basis points} * 182.5/360$$

And to convert annual basis points (30/360) to a semi-annual equivalent (actual/360):

$$(p.a. \text{ basis points} * 360/((1+(1+s.a. \text{ lending rate} * 182.5/360)) * 182.5)$$

Strictly speaking each of the loans could be valued at the forward forward rate for the appropriate period, but as these break even to the zero coupon equivalent maturity rate it is simpler to use this as a proxy for the forwards.

So taking the fixed-rate cash flows of the bond and the swap together:

	Bond cash flow	Swap cash flow
Net proceeds	99,825,000.00	
Year 1	−7,500,000.00	7,800,000.00
Year 2	−7,500,000.00	7,800,000.00
Year 3	−7,500,000.00	7,800,000.00
Year 4	−7,500,000.00	7,800,000.00
Year 4	−100,000,000.00	

If we combine the bond and swap cash flows, then we can see the borrower's net fixed-rate cash flow:

	Net cash flow
Net proceeds	99,825,000.00
Year 1	52,000.00
Year 2	52,000.00
Year 3	52,000.00
Year 4	52,000.00
Year 4	−100,000,000.00

The annual surplus arises as a result of the extent to which the bond issue is priced away from par (99.825%). The borrower could forgo the additional 52,000 each year by reducing the swap rate from 7.552% to 7.50% in return for an initial payment of the present value of 52,000 per annum.

If the discount rate used to calculate the present value was 7.552% (the borrower's 4-year cost of funds) then the present value would be 175,000 allowing for rounding errors, leaving the borrower with this structure:

Net proceeds	100,000,000
Years 1–4	Libor − 25 * 100,000,000
Year 4	−100,000,000

The swap counterparty is more likely however, to use a zero coupon curve to discount the cash flows. A margin is likely to be added to these rates as they are the rates at which the swap counterparty lends to the borrower for one, two, three and four years. Therefore 52,000 represents the repayment of principal and interest on four zero coupon loans. Using the following rates produces a present value of 99,995,252, assuming a margin of 1% above the zero curve for the loans:

	Swap curve	Zero curve
Year 1	7.100	7.100
Year 2	7.320	7.328
Year 3	7.610	7.638
Year 4	7.810	7.857

The difference of 4,748 is worth less than half a cent in price or 15/100 of one basis point in yield terms.

EUROPEANCORP

Amount	NOK 500,000,000
Maturity	Five years
Coupon	6.25% per annum
Issue price	100.5
Amortization	Bullet
Call option	If taxation changes (at par)
Listing	Luxembourg
Commissions	⅞%: management ¼%, underwriting ⅝%
Negative pledge	Yes
Cross default	Yes
Pari passu	Yes
Swap	To 6-month NOK Libor

Swap rates

	p.a. 30/360
1 year	5.50/60
2 year	5.75/85
3 year	6.10/20
4 year	6.30/40
5 year	6.70/80

Questions

1. What is Europeancorp's cost of floating-rate funds?

2. If a par/par structure is created using the borrower's cost of fixed-rate debt what impact does this have?

3. If a par/par structure is created using the 5-year swap rate what impact does this have?

4. If a par/par structure is created using a zero coupon curve what impact could this have?

1. In order to calculate the borrower's cost of floating-rate funds it is necessary to calculate the borrower's cost of fixed-rate funds, add the fixed-rate revenues from the swap (6.70% per annum, 30/360 on NOK 500,000,000), and express the difference in relation to the borrower's floating-rate swap payment of 6-month NOK Libor flat.

- cost of fixed-rate debt
- plus fixed-rate swap receipts
- minus floating-rate swap payments.

The borrower's cost of fixed-rate funds is a function of the net proceeds of the issue, the coupon payments and the redemption amount. The coupon payments are 6.25% of NOK 500,000,000 or NOK 31,250,000 and the redemption amount is par, or 100% of NOK 500,000,000, so the forward cash flows look like this:

Year 1	31,250,000.00
Year 2	31,250,000.00
Year 3	31,250,000.00
Year 4	31,250,000.00
Year 5	531,250,000.00

The net proceeds of the issue are calculated by deducting the commissions from the issue price:

Issue price	100.500%
less commissions	0.875%
Net proceeds	99.625%

and multiplying the result by the redemption amount of NOK 500,000,000 to produce NOK 498,125,000. So the borrower's cash flow looks like this:

Net proceeds	−498,125,000.00
Year 1	31,250,000.00
Year 2	31,250,000.00
Year 3	31,250,000.00
Year 4	31,250,000.00
Year 5	531,250,000.00

The minus sign indicates that the net proceeds represent cash flowing in a different direction from the coupon payments and the redemption amount. From the borrower's perspective the cash flow is positive and the subsequent cash flows are negative. Market participants often represent the cash flows as above because they require fewer key strokes for calculation than the real cash flows:

Net proceeds	498,125,000.00
Year 1	–31,250,000.00
Year 2	–31,250,000.00
Year 3	–31,250,000.00
Year 4	–31,250,000.00
Year 5	–531,250,000.00

They both produce an internal rate of return of 6.340%:

n	i	PV	PMT	FV
5	6.34	498,125,000.00	–31,250,000.00	–500,000,000.00

n	i	PV	PMT	FV
5	6.34	–498,125,000.00	31,250,000.00	500,000,000.00

The borrower's cost of fixed-rate debt is 6.34% per annum 30/360, and the swap receipt is 6.70% per annum 30/360.

- cost of fixed-rate debt
- plus fixed-rate swap receipts
- minus floating-rate swap payments.

The three component parts of the borrower's cost of floating-rate debt are established. It is now necessary to calculate the semi-annual equivalent of the difference between the revenue on the swap, 6.70% and the expenditure of the debt, 6.34%. In annual 30/360 terms the difference is 36 basis points. Discounting this to its semi-annual equivalent on an actual/360 basis gives 35 basis points.

To convert annual basis points (30/360) to a semi-annual equivalent (actual/360):

$$(\text{p.a. basis points} * 360/((1+(1+\text{s.a. lending rate}*182.5/360))*182.5)$$
$$(36 * 360/((1+(1+0.06591*182.5/360))*182.5)$$
$$= 35 \text{ basis points}$$

So the borrower's cost of funds on a floating-rate basis is 6-month NOK Libor minus 35 basis points or Libor minus 0.35%. This means that the borrower can choose between being paid 6.70% per annum in the swap and paying NOK Libor flat in return or receiving 6.34% and paying NOK Libor minus 35 basis points.

NOK 6.70%

Issuer

Swap counterparty

6-month NOK Libor flat

NOK 6.34%

Fig 5.4

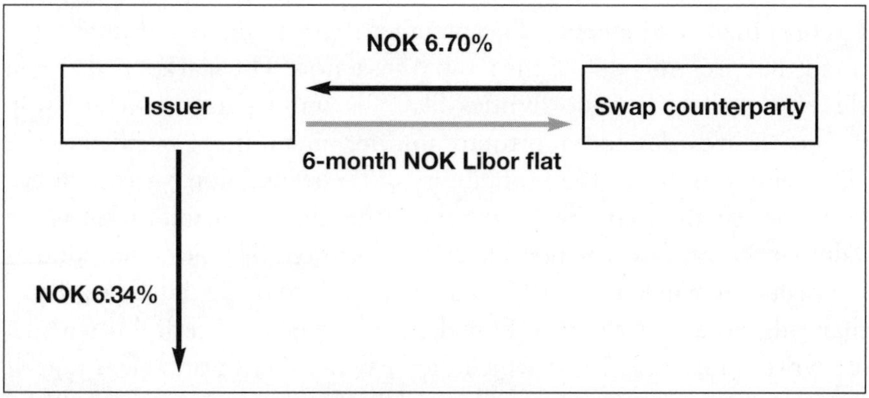

While the structure shown in Figure 5.4 is possible the vast majority of borrowers choose to match the cash flows of their bond issues with the cash flows of the swap. Effectively they are performing a netting operation in which each side of the transaction has the same value deducted from it. In this case the value is 35 (0.35%) semi-annual money market (actual/360) basis points or 36 (0.36%) annual bond basis points. The idea is that the same amount of cash in present value terms is deducted from each side of the swap transaction.

From the perspective of the market the swap has no value at the time the deal is struck. It is neither better to be a payer nor a receiver. There is no intrinsic advantage in either and there is therefore no intrinsic value in either side of the swap. On the contrary, if a swap was executed and reversed immediately, with no change in market prices, then it would cost the party the bid/offer spread. So it can be said that the value of the trade at the time the deal is struck is approximately zero, or more precisely the bid/offer spread. This is a positive value to a market maker and a cost to non-market makers.

> **The value of a swap at the time a deal is struck is approximately equal to zero.**

This is true of all transactions, subject to market liquidity. The wider the bid/offer spread the more expensive it is to cross the market, to buy and then sell, or to sell and then buy. The more efficient the market the closer its transaction value is to zero. Buying and selling a house, or a second hand car, could be an expensive exercise in terms of the bid/offer spread.

The value of a swap at the time a deal is struck is approximately equal to zero and for a market maker the actual value is equal to the bid offer spread. So when restructuring a swap transaction the market maker will be concerned with meeting the customer's requirement and improving on the net present value of the swap transaction. The market maker will therefore welcome opportunities like this one to restructure a swap because it provides an opportunity to offer an additional service to the client and to improve the profitability of the transaction for the bank.

In essence all swap structures follow the same principle: what is the value of the cash flow which the client has asked be paid? The value of the cash flow which the market maker will ask to be paid will be greater than this. So essentially market makers ask to be paid cash flows which are worth more than those which they pay out. This principle is not, of course, peculiar to the swap market. All transactions basically work in this way. If I exchange money from one currency to another I am basically selling cash flows to a market maker which are worth more than those which the market maker will pay to me.

> **Swaps market makers pay out less than they receive.**

This is therefore consistent with the way that other market makers earn a living and is simply another way of saying that the swap market maker aims to earn the bid/offer spread. The bid/offer spread is usually expressed in annual interest terms whereas a swap book is valued in present value terms.

So when the issuer pays Libor minus 35 basis points instead of Libor flat, and receives 6.34% instead of 6.70% the market maker is looking not so much at these gross flows, or the actual payments in the transaction, but more at the net value of the two flows expressed in present value terms.

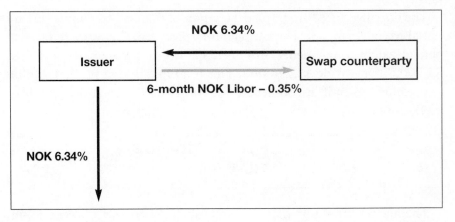

Fig 5.5

2. If a par/par structure is created then the borrower will be paid the cash flow which exactly matches its existing position. Here is the borrower's original cash flow from the bond issue:

Net proceeds	498,125,000.00
Year 1	–31,250,000.00
Year 2	–31,250,000.00
Year 3	–31,250,000.00
Year 4	–31,250,000.00
Year 5	–531,250,000.00

In order to match this flow the borrower needs to receive those cash flows which will leave it with 100% proceeds at the start of the deal and 100% repayment at the end of the deal. Hence the term "par/par structure": receiving a par amount at drawdown and paying a par amount at maturity.

The borrower needs to receive 1,875,000 at the start of the deal and when this is added to the net proceeds it results in a combined payment to the borrower of NOK 500,000,000. The annual payments required to meet the coupon payments are NOK 31,250,000 so the cash flow which creates a par/par structure looks like this:

Year 0	1,875,000.00
Year 1	31,250,000.00
Year 2	31,250,000.00
Year 3	31,250,000.00
Year 4	31,250,000.00
Year 5	31,250,000.00

The borrower needs to be paid a coupon of 6.25% per annum plus an initial payment of ⅜%. The swap counterparty can therefore reduce its annual coupon payments from 6.34% to 6.25% or from NOK 31,700,000 to NOK 31,250,000. This is a reduction of NOK 450,000 per annum which if discounted at the borrower's all-in cost of funds is NOK 1,878,158.70.

n	i	PV	PMT	FV
5	6.34	−1,878,158.70	450,000.00	0.00

The answer would be more accurate if the borrower's precise all-in cost was used to calculate the swap cash flows and as a discount rate:

n	i	PV	PMT	FV
5	6.339848	−1,874,994.41	449,240.00	0.00

In order to produce an answer exactly equal to NOK 1,875,000 it would be necessary to calculate the swap cash flows and the discount rate precisely. Adding another decimal to the discount rate produces an answer of NOK 1,875,000.66:

n	i	PV	PMT	FV
5	6.3398483	−1,874,000.66	449,241.50	0.00

There is therefore no financial impact of creating a par/par structure using the borrower's cost of funds as the discount rate.

3. If the swap rate is used as a discount rate the net proceeds will be a little less than if the borrower's cost of funds is used because the swap rate is higher. This means that the borrower will not have sufficient funds to top up the net proceeds to the par amount. If a par/par structure is required it is necessary to consider whether the difference between the value of the net proceeds discounted at the borrower's cost of funds and the swap rate is significant enough to influence the cost of funds. One basis point annually on NOK 500,000,000 is equal to NOK 50,000 per annum. This has a present value of about NOK 206,667:

n	i	PV	PMT	FV
5	6.70	−206,667.21	50,000.00	0.00

The initial payment from the swap counterparty to the borrower calculated at the borrower's cost of funds is NOK 1,878,158.70:

n	i	PV	PMT	FV
5	6.34	−1,878,158.70	450,000.00	0.00

The initial payment from the swap counterparty to the borrower calculated at the swap rate is NOK 1,860,000. The difference of about NOK 20,000 per annum is not significant enough to influence the borrower's cost of floating-rate funds.

4. The swap counterparty could treat the initial payment to the borrower as a series of zero coupon loans which are repaid in reduced fixed-rate swap payments each year. There are therefore five zero coupon loans with maturities of one, two, three, four and five years. Since the swap counterparty is lending money a strong case can be made for discounting these cash flows not at the borrower's cost of funds, or even at the swap rate, but at the bank's lending rate for a borrower of this credit quality and these maturities. In practice there are a number of other considerations. Is the bank the lead manager of the issue? If so, to what extent is the bond issue expected to be profitable? What is the margin on the swap transaction? Does the swap give the bank a good trading position? Can the swap be used for marketing purposes to make attractive offers to clients and prospects?

In answering these questions the bank will be able to put the cost of the different values resulting from different discount rates into perspective. It is not usually regarded as a single item issue but as part of a range of issues which need to be considered when structuring a package which includes a swap.

Currency swap

IBM AND THE WORLD BANK (INTERNATIONAL BANK FOR RECONSTRUCTION & DEVELOPMENT)

CASE STUDY

CHF	D-mark
12,375,00	30,000,000
12,375,00	30,000,000
12,375,00	30,000,000
12,375,00	30,000,000
212,375,00	330,000,000

These flows represent IBM's outstanding debt. IBM had issued bonds in both Swiss francs and D-marks prior to entering into the swap transaction with the World Bank.

The World Bank agreed to pay 8% and 11% to IBM in the swap transaction for CHF and D-marks respectively. IBM agreed to service the World Bank's US$ borrowing which had a coupon of 16% p.a. 30/360. Assume that the combined value of the CHF and D-mark flows (to the nearest $1,000) is equivalent to the net proceeds of the World Bank's US$ bond issue. Fees for the new issue were 2%. The issue price was par. The spot foreign exchange rates were:

US$/CHF: 2.2000
US$/D-mark: 2.5872

Questions

1. How much did IBM pay in US$ to the World Bank each year?

2. What was the final exchange of principal?

3. Why was no initial exchange of principal necessary?

4. What benefits were there for the World Bank in completing this transaction?

5. What benefits were there for IBM in completing this transaction?

Answers

1. Discount the CHF cash flow at the rate the World Bank is prepared to pay (8%). Follow the same procedure for the D-mark cash flow at 11%. Convert these amounts to US$ at their spot rates and add them together:

n	i	PV	PMT	FV
5	8	-185,526,426.00	12,375,000.00	200,000,000.00

CHF PV = 185,526,426
at 2.20
= US$ 84,330,194

So the value of the Swiss franc cash flows which IBM wants to be paid by the World Bank is CHF 185,526,426 or in dollar terms US$ 84,330,194 (CHF 185,526,426/2.20). This is effectively the mark-to-market value of IBM's debt. The coupon in Swiss francs on IBM's bond issue was 6³⁄₁₆% (12,375,000/200,000,000 *100) so IBM had borrowed Swiss francs in a lower interest rate environment. Now Swiss francs rates are about 8% so IBM is effectively locking in an interest rate gain when executing the swap transaction with the World Bank. That is why the value of the Swiss franc cash flow has fallen from 200,000,000 to 185,526,426:

n	i	PV	PMT	FV
5	11	288,912,309.00	30,000,000.00	300,000,000.00

$$\text{D-mark PV} = 288{,}912{,}309$$
$$\text{at } 2.5872$$
$$= \text{US\$ } 111{,}669{,}878$$

The mark-to-market value of IBM's D-mark bond issue is D-mark 288,912,309. IBM originally issued D-mark 300,000,000 with a coupon of 10% (30,000,000/300,000,000 * 100). D-mark interest rates have now moved up to about 11% and IBM is using the swap trans-action as a way of locking in an interest rate gain. This is why the mark-to-market value of their mark cash flows is lower than the amount originally borrowed.

$$\text{Total PV} = \text{US\$ } 196{,}000{,}072$$
$$(\text{US\$ } 111{,}669{,}878 + \text{US\$ } 84{,}330{,}194)$$

So the combined mark-to-market value of the two IBM cash flows is US$ 196,000,)72 or US$ 196,000,000 to the nearest US$ 1,000.

This represents the net proceeds of the bond issue and since the fees are 2% it must therefore represent 98% of the issue amount since we are told that the issue price is par. If US$ 196,000,000 represents 98% of the issue then 100% of the issue is US$ 200,000,000:

$$\text{Total PV} = \text{US\$ } 196{,}000{,}000 * 100/98$$
$$= \text{US\$ } 200{,}000{,}000$$

The coupon on bond issue is 16% or US$ 32,000,000. So IBM's dollar payments to the World Bank were:

	IBM's US$ swap payments
Year 1	32,000,000.00
Year 2	32,000,000.00
Year 3	32,000,000.00
Year 4	32,000,000.00
Year 5	232,000,000.00

2. In the final exchange of principal IBM paid US$ 200,000,000 to the World Bank and the World Bank paid CHF 200,000,000 and D-mark 300,000,000. These are the cash flows necessary for the two parties to service their existing debt. IBM's objective was to change Swiss franc and D-mark debt to dollar debt. In order to achieve this it was necessary for IBM to have exactly matching cash flows in Swiss francs and D-marks. In this way IBM created a fully hedged transaction.

IBM has exactly matching cash flows in the Swiss franc swap and in the Swiss franc bond issue. The swap payments mirror the bond payments.

CHF bond issue	CHF swap receipts
−12,375,000	12,375,000
−12,375,000	12,375,000
−12,375,000	12,375,000
−12,375,000	12,375,000
−212,375,000	212,375,000

The same is true in D-marks, the cash flows of the swap exactly match those of the bond issue.

D-mark bond issue	D-mark swap receipts
−30,000,000	30,000,000
−30,000,000	30,000,000
−30,000,000	30,000,000
−30,000,000	30,000,000
−330,000,000	330,000,000

So in order to match the cash flows of the bond issues precisely it is necessary for IBM to receive D-mark 300,000,000 and CHF 200,000,000 at the final exchange of principal.

3. It is usual practice in the inter-bank market to have an exchange of principal both at the start of a currency swap and at the end. Where a market maker deals with a client however, the initial exchange of principal is a matter of choice for the client: if the client wants to have an initial exchange that's fine, but if they decide not to then the market maker will oblige. The final exchange of principal in a currency swap is a vital part of the transaction but the initial exchange is optional.

> **The final exchange of principal in a currency swap is a vital part of the transaction.**

> **The initial exchange of principal is optional in client driven transactions.**

If a client chooses not to exchange principal at the start of the transaction it is a simple matter for the market maker to use the spot foreign exchange market to cover any exposure. This is not of course possible with the final exchange. The principal governing the structuring of currency swaps is the same as that which governs interest rate swaps:

> **The market maker in a currency swap pays cash flows which are worth less than those it receives.**

So the guiding principle is to calculate in present value terms the cash flows paid by one party in a swap and compare them with the present value of the cash flows paid by the other party. In the case of IBM and the World Bank they are each paying cash flows which in present value terms are worth US$ 196,000,000.

No initial exchange was necessary in this case because IBM had no funds to exchange. IBM had already used the proceeds of the Swiss franc and D-mark bond issues in its business. What IBM wanted was to change its debt into dollars. From the World Bank's perspective an absence of an initial exchange was acceptable because it could use the spot market to convert the dollar proceeds of its issue into Swiss francs and D-marks.

4. The World Bank benefited from this transaction because it was able to create cheaper Swiss franc debt and D-mark debt by swapping a dollar issue than it could have by issuing Swiss francs and D-marks directly. They also received very favorable press coverage in the *Wall Street Journal* and the *Financial Times* as a result of the transaction. The publicity gave an enormous boost to a market which had been regarded with an amount of suspicion by some of the potential participants. If this market was acceptable to IBM and the World Bank in a deal which became public then there was unlikely to be any fundamental flaw in the process. Since the World Bank became an active user of the market it could be argued that they contributed to creating liquidity by encouraging others to become players in the swap market.

5. IBM benefited from this transaction by locking in the interest rate gains in Swiss francs ($8\% - 6\frac{3}{16}\%$) and D-marks ($11\% - 10\%$). There was also a currency gain because the Swiss franc and the D-mark had weakened against the dollar since IBM issued the Swiss franc and D-mark bonds. So IBM was able to use the currency swap to lock in both interest rate and currency gains. It is worth noting that the swap does not create the gains, it is simply a tool for capturing them. The decision to borrow in a foreign currency creates the potential for a currency gain or loss and the decision to borrow on a fixed-rate basis creates the opportunity for an interest rate gain or loss.

Currency swaps

CASE STUDY

NORDIC EXPORT CREDIT

Amount	NOK 500 million
Maturity	3 years
Coupon	6.00%
Issue price	101¼%
Amortization	Bullet
Call option	None
Listing	Luxembourg
Denominations	NOK 1,000, NOK 10,000, NOK 100,000
Commissions	1⅜%
Expenses	NOK 50,000
Stabilization	IPMA
Swap	Into floating-rate US$
Governing law	English
Negative pledge	Yes
Cross default	Yes
Pari passu	Yes
Rating	AAA/Aaa

Market comment

The pricing of this Triple A name was considered fair, but demand was slower than might have been expected, partly because of the Friday afternoon timing, ahead of a long weekend in London – traders manifested little desire to spend their holiday weekends worrying about positions. It remained within full fees, however, and should trade up further next week. The deal was swapped into floating-rate US dollars at around 35 bp under Libor, better than market rates at the time.

Spot US$/NOK: 7.50
NOK 3-year interest rate swap: 6.46/51
US$/NOK basis swap: +3/–5 (against 6-month US$ Libor flat)

1. What are the net proceeds of the issue?

2. Who pays the fees and expenses in a bond issue?

3. When are they paid?

4. What is the borrower's cost of fixed-rate NOK?

5. Write out in cash terms the borrower's cash flow resulting from the issue of fixed-rate krone.

6. Draw a diagram showing the direction of the borrower's cash flows in a Norwegian krone interest rate swap, swapping the fixed-rate bond issue to a floating-rate basis.

7. What is the borrower's all-in cost of floating-rate krone after entering into the swap transaction?

8. What initial, or up front, payment does the borrower need to receive in order to create a par/par structure?

9. What annual swap payment does the borrower need to receive in order to create a par/par structure.

10. Show the fixed-rate cash flows of the bond and the swap and the net fixed-rate cash flows resulting from the creation of a par/par structure.

11. Show the two possible transactions which could result from a market maker's quote of a basis swap price of US$/NOK +3/–5 (against 6-month US$ Libor flat).

12. Show the direction of the cash flows if the borrower swaps from floating-rate krone to floating-rate dollars.

13. What is the borrower's net cost of floating-rate dollars if the swap counterparty agrees to match the borrower's cash flow in floating-rate krone?

14. What does "better than market rates at the time" mean?

15. What is a cross-default clause?

16. What does *pari passu* mean?

17. What is a negative pledge?

1. The borrower receives net proceeds of NOK 499,325,000.

The proceeds of the issue are NOK 499,375,000 (99.875% of the redemption amount NOK 500,000,000). The issue price is 101.25% and from this the commissions of 1.375% need to be deducted, which leaves 99.875% from which the expenses are deducted.

2. All the fees and expenses in the issue are for the account of the borrower.

3. They are paid as a deduction from the issue price.

Issue price	101.250%		
Commissions	1.375%		
Proceeds	99.875%	* 500,000,000 =	499,375,000.00
		Less expenses	50,000.00
		Net proceeds	499,325,000.00

4. The borrower's cost of fixed-rate NOK is 6.051%. The redemption amount is NOK 500,000,000, the coupon is NOK 30,000,000 (NOK 500,000,000 * 6%) and the net proceeds are NOK 499,325,000. Remember that some calculators require that one of the cash flows is different in direction from the others in order to establish an internal rate of return or an all-in cost.

n	i	PV	PMT	FV
3	6.051	−499,325,000	30,000,000.00	500,000,000.00

5. So the borrower's cash flow in NOK looks like this:

Year 0	499,325,000.00
Year 1	−30,000,000.00
Year 2	−30,000,000.00
Year 3	−530,000,000.00
All-in cost	6.051

6. If the borrower swaps the bond issue from fixed- to floating-rate NOK then the transaction would be as shown in Figure 5.6.

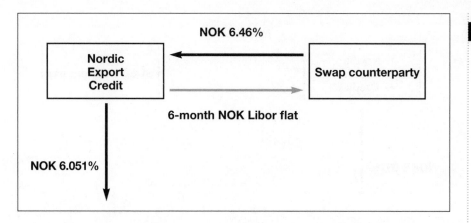

Fig 5.6

7. If Nordic Export Credit swaps this from a fixed- to a floating-rate basis then its all-in cost of floating-rate NOK would be 6-month NOK Libor minus 40 basis points (6-month NOK Libor – 0.40%).

This is calculated by discounting the difference between the swap receipt and the all-in cost of the bond issue, 40.9 basis points (6.46 – 6.051), to its present value:

n	i	PV	PMT	FV
3	6.46	−108.40	40.90	0.00

The result, 108.4 basis points flat, is then compounded on a semi-annual money market basis at the semi-annual equivalent rate to 6.46% per annum, which is 6.359%.

n	i	PV	PMT	FV
3	6.359/2	−108.40		0.00

This compounds to 20.13 basis points in each semi-annual period. This needs to be expressed on a money market basis as 19.85 basis points and doubled to 39.7 basis points to comply with the market convention for quoting semi-annual rates. Rounded to the nearest basis point the result is NOK Libor minus 40 basis points.

This can be cross-checked using this formula:

p.a. basis points * 360/((1+((1+(s.a. lending rate*182.5/360)))*182.5)

40.9 *360/((1 + ((1 + (0.06359 * 182.5/360))) * 182.5) = 39.7 basis points

Fig 5.7

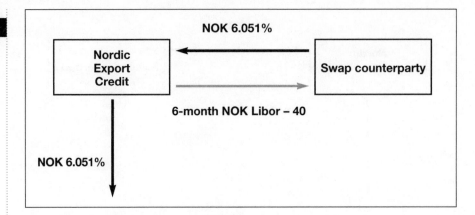

Fig 5.8

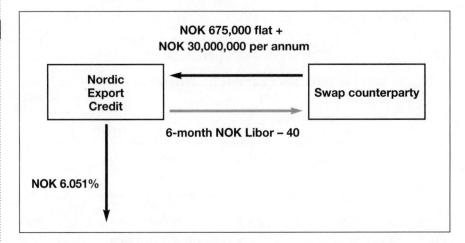

8. & 9. After structuring the deal as shown in Figures 5.7 and 5.8, with an initial payment of NOK 675,000 and an annual payment of NOK 30,000,000 the borrower has a net fixed-rate cash flow of NOK 500,00,000 at the start of the transaction and NOK 500,000,000 at the end. The borrower is therefore able to draw down the par amount, pay 6-month NOK Libor minus 40 on the par amount and repay the par amount. Hence the market terminology which sometimes refers to these transactions as par/par structures. The same phenomenon exists in the asset swap market.

10.

	Bond	Swap	Net fixed
Year 0	499,325,000.00	675,000.00	500,000,000.00
Year 1	−30,000,000.00	30,000,000.00	
Year 2	−30,000,000.00	30,000,000.00	
Year 3	−530,000,000.00	30,000,000.00	−500,000,000.00
All-in cost	6.051		

11.

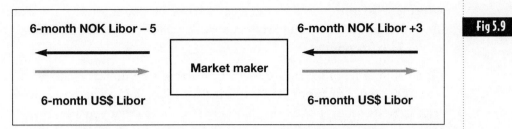

Fig 5.9

Nordic Export Credit needs to receive floating-rate Norwegian krone to match its floating-rate debt generated through the interest rate swap from fixed-rate krone. So in the basis swap the borrower will receive 6-month NOK Libor minus 5 basis points and pay 6-month US$ Libor flat.

12.

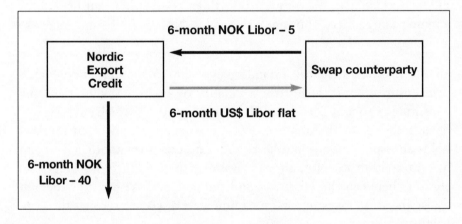

Fig 5.10

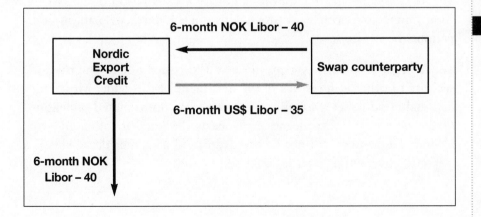

Fig 5.11

This can be restructured, subject to the swap counterparty's agreement to produce matching cash flows in floating-rate krone at Libor minus 40 and a net payment in dollars at 6-month US$ Libor minus 35 basis points.

13. Swapping from fixed-rate NOK to floating-rate dollars changes the borrower's cost of funds to 6-month US$ Libor –35. The basis swap price is NOK Libor +3/ NOK Libor –5. This means that a market maker will pay NOK Libor –5 in order to receive 6-month US$ Libor flat, and needs to be paid NOK Libor +3 in return for 6-month US$ Libor flat.

14. "Better than market rates at the time" means that if the borrower had entered into this transaction at the market swap rates prevailing at the time the deal was struck it would not have been possible to achieve a cost of funds as low as NOK Libor minus 35. Sometimes new issues come to the market because there is a very aggressive payer in the swap market, willing to pay a higher fixed rate than the bid side of the market. Bidders are sometimes willing to do this because they can be sure of winning a large piece of business in one hit. Not dissimilar in concept to a discount for a large order.

15. A cross-default clause, a standard covenant in an international bond issue ensures that if the borrower defaults on one transaction then that constitutes an act of default on all other transactions which have a cross-default clause. In the absence of a cross-default clause if an investor holds an issuer's bonds and hears about a default on another issue but has no coupon due for, say six months, then there is no breach of contract between the borrower and the investor. With a cross-default clause the same investor can take immediate action to recover the non-payment of interest.

16. *Pari passu* means that all the bonds rank equally so no investor has an advantage over other investors. This is a standard covenant in international bond issues.

17. A negative pledge is a promise by the issuer not to improve the security of other bond issues to the detriment of this issue. Most international bond issues are senior, unsecured, unsubordinated obligations of the borrower and a negative pledge is designed to offer investors assurance that they will not be disadvantaged at a later date. This is a standard covenant in international bond issues.

Swapping from fixed to fixed

If a customer wants to swap from a fixed-rate basis in one currency to a fixed-rate basis in another currency it is possible for the transaction to be structured for them as one deal. In reality the swap counterparty may enter into three transactions in order to hedge a fixed/fixed swap, two interest rate swaps and a basis swap, but the product of these can be presented to the client as one deal. If, for example a customer wants to swap from fixed-rate yen to fixed-rate dollars then they would have the following trade:

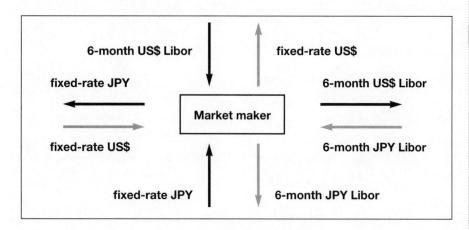

Fig 5.12

The market maker could hedge this transaction by entering into an interest rate swap in yen, an interest rate swap in dollars and a basis swap between floating-rate yen and floating-rate dollars. In the yen interest rate swap the market maker would be a receiver of fixed and a payer of floating. In the dollar interest rate swap the market maker would be a payer of fixed and a receiver of floating. In the basis swap the market maker would be a payer of floating-rate dollar interest and a receiver of floating-rate yen interest.

Fig 5.13

Asset and Liability Management

Overview

Swaps are used extensively as a tool for asset and liability management and this chapter explores some of the more commonly used applications of this technique. These include using currency swaps to diversify a bank's loan book; locking in currency gains and losses in the swap market; using currency swaps to diversify institutional investors' portfolios and the use of asset swaps. It outlines the use of swaps for changing the risk exposure of assets and liabilities which have commodity, equity or credit risk embedded within them. There are exercises on the calculation of currency gains and losses and on various aspects of the asset swap market including the calculation of a bond price from an investor's asset swap target and the calculation of a break-even swap rate given a bond price and an investor's target floating-rate return.

Introduction

Banks have traditionally taken deposits from their customers and put those deposits to work as loans. Because the deposits and the loans are denominated in the same currency, this activity has no associated foreign exchange risk. But it does limit banks to lending to customers which need to borrow in the currencies which the bank has available on deposit.

If a bank is asked to lend to a customer in a currency other than one of those it has on deposit it creates a currency exposure for the bank. Suppose a customer wants to borrow euros from a US bank for five years and that the US bank has no natural source of euros. It is possible for the bank to cover this exposure in the forward market by selling euros forward and buying US dollars. The transaction costs associated with this, in particular the bid/offer spread in the medium-term foreign exchange forward market, would make the resultant cost of the loan prohibitively expensive for the borrower.

Currency swaps provide an economic alternative to this problem for banks. In order to cover the exposure created by a loan to a customer in euros funded by a bank's deposit in US dollars, a bank could receive fixed-rate US dollars in a currency swap and pay fixed-rate euros.

One of the consequences of the development of the currency swap market is that banks now often make much more competitive medium-term forward foreign exchange prices than they used to. Most banks quote forward foreign exchange and currency swap prices from the same desk and increased liquidity in the latter has improved liquidity in the former. Banks therefore, need no longer restrict their lending activities to the currencies in which they have natural deposits. They are free to fund themselves in the most competitively priced currency and to lend to their customers in the currency of the customer's preference, using a currency swap as an asset and liability matching tool.

Locking in currency gains and losses

If a fixed-rate loan is marked to market it is possible to say to what extent the loan is "in the money" or "out of the money," that is to say, the extent to which the loan's value is lower than or higher than the current price for a new loan for the same borrower for the same term.

If a company has a 3-year outstanding loan at 5% per annum, drawn down two years ago as a 5-year facility we can mark the loan to market by asking the price at which the customer could borrow for three years in today's market. If the price is 6% per annum, then we can say that the mark-to-market gain is 1% per annum. The customer has a loan which is priced 1% below the current market price, so the loan is "in the money" by 1% per annum. So on a loan of US$ 100 million, this would be worth US$ 1 million per annum. At a discount rate of 6% per annum, this has a value of US$ 2,673,011.95. Or we could say that the approximate present value of 1% per annum for three years at a discount rate of 6% is 2.673%.

Year 1	1,000,000.00	1.06	943,396.23
Year 2	1,000,000.00	1.06^2	889,996.44
Year 3	1,000,000.00	1.06^3	839,619.28
			2,673,011.95

This mark-to-market gain is on an opportunity basis only. This means that the borrower could make further gains if interest rates continue to rise or that the existing gain could be reduced if interest rates fall. Indeed, if rates fall below 5% per annum, then the gain will become a loss.

If the borrower wants to realize the gain, then it is necessary to enter into a transaction which locks in the benefit. This means that the opportunity to make further gains will be eliminated at the same time as the possibility of making losses or of suffering a reduction in the gain.

If this gain is in the borrower's base currency, the currency in which it reports its accounts to shareholders, then the gain can be said to be an interest rate gain. If, on the other hand, the gain is in a foreign currency then it is subject to increase, if the currency appreciates, or decrease, if the currency depreciates. This is one source of currency gains and losses.

A much larger potential gain or loss in currency terms arises when a borrower draws down unhedged debt in a foreign currency. If the foreign currency appreciates, then the base currency value of the borrowing increases and the loan becomes more expensive to repay. If the £/US$ spot rate is 1.65 and a UK company borrows US$ 100,000,000, then its mark-to-market value at drawdown is £60,606,060.61:

$$US\$\ 100,000,000/1.65$$
$$= £60,606,060.61$$

If the US dollar strengthens to, say 1.40 then the mark-to-market value of the loan becomes £71,428,571.43:

$$US\$ \ 100,000,000/1.40$$
$$= £71,428,571.43$$

So on a mark-to-market basis the borrower has made an opportunity loss of £10,822,510.82 (£71,428,571.43 – £60,606,060.61).

For this loss to become real and fixed it would be necessary for the borrower to cover the dollar/sterling exchange rate risk. So locking in currency gains and losses is very similar in concept to locking in interest rate gains and losses and in fact the two often happen simultaneously.

IBM'S CURRENCY SWAPS WITH THE WORLD BANK

EXAMPLE

IBM's motivation in entering into its celebrated currency swaps with the World Bank (see Chapter 5) was fueled by its desire to lock in both interest rate gains and currency gains. IBM had borrowed Swiss francs and D-marks, converting the proceeds of its debt to dollars. This created two risks: the first an exposure to interest rates, since it was fixed-rate debt; the second to currency exposure, since dollars would be used to repay the bond issues. Executing the swaps enabled IBM to lock in gains resulting from favorable interest rate and currency movements. IBM could also have realized these gains in the forward foreign exchange market. Liquidity in the forward foreign exchange market would not however have resulted in a price competitive with the cost of the swap. IBM used the swap to create cheap dollar debt.

Here is IBM's outstanding cash flow in D-marks. The cash flows look like those generated by a fixed coupon of 10% on a bullet issue of D-mark 300,000,000. So if IBM is paid 11% in a swap, its interest rate gain is 1% per annum or, in present value terms is 3.696% if the discount rate is also 11%.

	D-marks
Year 1	30,000,000.00
Year 2	30,000,000.00
Year 3	30,000,000.00
Year 4	30,000,000.00
Year 5	330,000,000.00

Question

How much is IBM's currency gain or loss?

Answer

In order to calculate this we need to look at the exchange rate movement between the dollar and the D-mark from the time that IBM issued the D-marks bonds to the time when it locked in this gain by executing the currency swaps with the World Bank.

If the US$/D-mark exchange rate was 2.5785 at the time of the swap transaction then the redemption value of the US$ debt would have been US$ 116,346,713.21. So this is effectively the amount of debt which IBM will repay. The foreign currency gain is the difference between this amount and the amount which IBM originally borrowed. If the exchange rate at the time the bond was issued was, for example, US$/D-mark 2.20, then the currency gain would have been US$ 20,016,923.16.

D-mark		US$
300,000,000.00	2.5785	116,346,713.21
300,000,000.00	2.2000	136,363,636.36
		20,016,923.16

Credit arbitrage: IBM's cost of funds

IBM also locked in a gain resulting from credit arbitrage:

All-in cost of bond issue:	D-mark – 10.90%
Swap receipt:	D-mark + 11.00%
Swap payment:	US$ – 16.80%
Net cost (approximately):	US$ – 16.70%

The total gains, IBM's 10 basis points and the World Bank's 20 basis points are equal to and originate from their funding differentials.

Funding differentials set the boundaries of the swap price between counterparties. There is therefore an implied ceiling and floor for swap prices between which the demand for fixed-rate money and its supply, often in the form of bond issues, fluctuates.

Changing an investor's portfolio currency mix

Swaps are used as a method of changing the mix of fixed- and floating-rate debt in a borrower's funding book, and to change the mix of fixed- and floating-rate investments in a fund manager's portfolio. Neither of these operations involves changing the underlying portfolios. This means that the borrowers and investors who use swaps to alter their risk profiles do not actually need to change their underlying borrowing or their investments. It is the saving of the transaction costs associated with these activities which make the swap such a popular risk management tool.

The same technique can of course be extended across currencies. A fund manager wishing to reduce the firm's exposure over the next two years to Japan for example, and increase the firm's exposure to say, Europe, could sell yen-denominated investments and buy euro-denominated investments. This transaction would have the disadvantage that the fund manager would incur the costs of the bid/offer spread when switching back to yen. There are sometimes other difficulties associated with this. There may not always be sufficient liquidity to ensure a competitive bid for the yen assets.

There is a potential solution to these difficulties. The fund manager could keep the yen-denominated investments but hedge away the currency risk and create a corresponding risk in euros. This could involve, for example, receiving fixed-rate yen in a currency swap and paying euros.

At the maturity of the swap the investor has the same underlying exposure as was the case before the swap. This means that there are no bid/offer spreads to be paid, as would have been the case if the yen investment had been sold, a euro-equivalent investment purchased and then the transaction reversed two years later with the sale of the euro investment and the repurchase of the yen-denominated investment.

Market making and trading

The development of currency swaps can be traced to several sources, one of which is the capital market arbitrage created and exploited by the world's best-rated borrower as much today as in the late 1970s and the early 1980s, albeit at tighter spreads and therefore for smaller gains. It was not always therefore the case that currency swap pricing was coincident with forward foreign exchange pricing. Many of the original market participants were only players in either the bond market or the swap market and even for those firms with a presence in both there were sometimes communication gaps between the desks in question.

There were therefore arbitrage opportunities available as currency swaps and forward foreign exchange forwards are economically equivalent with different packaging and accounting mechanisms. Essentially the interest differential in a forward foreign exchange contact is netted between the two currencies, rolled up and paid on a zero coupon basis at the maturity of the trade. Currency swaps often settle the interest rate differentials between the currencies in question on a gross basis at least annually.

From a trading perspective this means that banks could take long positions in currencies by either receiving the currency in a currency swap or by buying the currency forward. Short positions could be taken by reversing this process, paying fixed in a swap or selling the currency in the forward market.

As the markets became more competitive in the 1980s many banks reorganized their currency activities so that both forward foreign exchange prices and currency swap prices were quoted by the same desk if not the same trader. From a trading perspective this helped to boost the liquidity in both markets resulting in narrower bid/offer spreads than had been the case. The liquidity provided by these merged desks substantially increased the possibilities for borrowers and investors to hedge their medium-term currency positions while at the same time producing opportunities for banks to run positions on the back of their customer order flow.

Capital adequacy considerations constrain this business, reducing the returns on capital available to banks for taking currency positions but the requirements of market making ensure that it is not always possible for an active market maker to run its book on a matched basis.

Asset swaps

Asset swaps are an application of currency and interest rate swaps rather than a different concept. Each of the transactions we have considered involved swapping debt. These swaps are liability swaps. When swap traders and arrangers talk about swaps, they usually refer to liability swaps simply as swaps and use the term "asset swap," or "asset swap package," to differentiate asset swaps from liability swaps. Asset swaps involve swapping investments. Liability swaps involve swapping debt.

Asset swaps change investments. Liability swaps change debt.

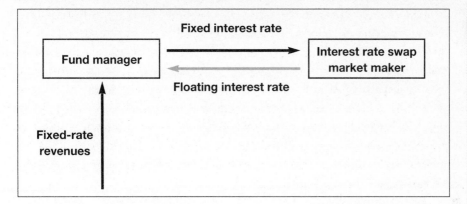

Fig 6.1

An 8% 3-year bond issued by a bank has the following cash flows:

Year	
0	−10,000,000.00
1	800,000.00
2	800,000.00
3	10,800,000.00

A German bank wants to buy the bond, but the bank wants to fund this investment on a floating-rate basis and therefore requires a return on a floating-rate basis from the 8% bond. So the German bank decides to buy the bond and simultaneously enter into an interest rate swap in which the bank will pay away the fixed-rate revenues from the bond and will in return receive floating-rate revenues from an interest rate swap market maker (see Figure 6.2).

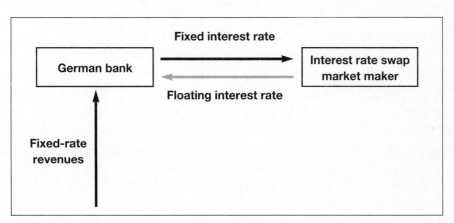

Fig 6.2

The German bank still owns the fixed-rate bond and still has an exposure to the credit risk on the bond. Having entered into an interest rate swap the bank has, however, changed the nature of its interest rate exposure. Prior to entering into the swap, the bank, as a holder of a fixed-rate bond, was exposed to changes in fixed rates of interest, so if interest rates went down the value of the bond would go up. If interest rates rose, then the price of the bond would fall. After executing the interest rate swap, the bank has changed its exposure to interest rates. Now if rates rise the bank receives higher revenues, if rates fall the bank receives lower revenues. The bank has however decided to fund this purchase by borrowing in the money markets on a floating-rate basis. So the German bank's assets, the bond plus the swap, match its liabilities, its funding in the money markets.

The yield available on the bond, if it is sold at par is 8% per annum 30/360. If the German bank enters into an interest rate swap transaction and pays 8% per annum 30/360 to the swap market maker in return for 6-month Libor flat, then the German bank's net revenue is 6-month Libor flat (see Figure 6.3).

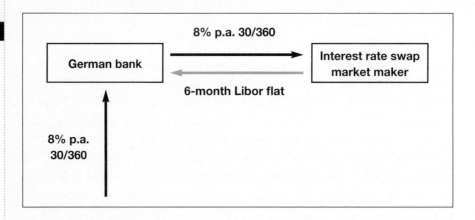

Fig 6.3

In practice, of course the purchaser of the bond combined with the swap will only be willing to buy the package if the yield is greater than that available on the cash market equivalent security, where one exists. In this example therefore the bank will want to know what yield is available on a 3-year floating-rate note for the same issuer. In practice, of course there may not be any existing floating-rate debt for this particular borrower and so one of the benefits of asset swaps is that they provide investors with a wider range of floating-rate investments than are available through the FRN market.

If a floater of the same maturity, issued by the same borrower does exist and its yield is Libor plus 10 basis points, then the German bank is unlikely to want to enter into an asset swap which produces a yield of Libor flat.

If the swap rate is lower than the yield on the bond, then the return available on a floating-rate basis is greater than Libor.

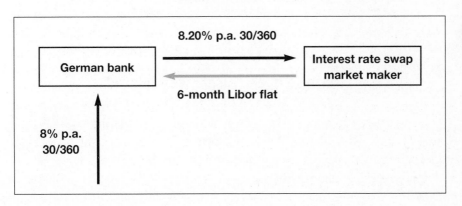

7.80% p.a. 30/360

German bank

Interest rate swap market maker

6-month Libor flat

8% p.a. 30/360

Fig 6.4

> **If a swap rate is lower than a corresponding bond yield then an asset swap package will produce a return above Libor.**

In this example the German bank receives a yield of 8% from the bond and pays 7.80% to the interest rate swap market maker (see Figure 6.4). The net of this revenue and expenditure is 20 basis points. This can be added to the floating-rate revenue paid by the swap market maker. So the total revenue received by the German bank is Libor plus about 20 basis points. In practice, it is necessary to make a small adjustment to the cash flows as the 20 basis point differential on a fixed-rate basis is annual 30/360 and the floating rate is semi-annual act/360.

If the swap rate is higher than the yield available on the bond, then the return available on a floating-rate basis is lower than Libor.

8.20% p.a. 30/360

German bank

Interest rate swap market maker

6-month Libor flat

8% p.a. 30/360

Fig 6.5

> If a swap rate is higher than a corresponding bond yield then an asset swap package will produce a return below Libor.

In the example shown in Figure 6.5 the German bank has the same revenue, 8% per annum 30/360, but the swap rate is 8.20% per annum 30/360. The net of the revenue and expenditure results in a cost of 20 basis points (per annum 30/360). When added to the floating-rate revenue in the swap at 6-month Libor flat the German bank has an all-in return of about Libor minus 20 basis points.

This process is a mirror of the new issue arbitrage process. In new issue arbitrage the revenue is generated by the swap and the expenditure by the bond issue. If the swap rate is higher than the all-in cost of issuing the bonds, then the issuer creates funds at a sub-Libor level. In an asset swap the revenue is generated by the yield on the fixed-rate bond and the expenditure by paying a fixed rate in an interest rate swap. If the revenue exceeds the expenditure the investor creates an asset swap package with a return above Libor.

This is not the only parallel between the new issue arbitrage process and the asset swap market. In new issue arbitrage, borrowers issue fixed-rate debt and swap it to a floating-rate basis because it produces a lower cost of floating-rate funds than would otherwise be available.

In an asset swap package, the investor swaps the fixed-rate cash flows of a bond to a floating-rate basis because it produces a higher return than would otherwise be available. A good understanding of the mechanics of the new issue arbitrage process is a good foundation for an understanding of the complexities of the structuring of asset swaps.

> Asset swaps can offer investors higher yields than those available in the FRN market.

Liquidity in the asset swap market

There are of course structural differences between owning an FRN and owning an asset swap. Investors often buy asset swap packages containing both a fixed-rate bond and a matching interest rate swap which effectively changes the revenue stream of the bond to a floating-rate basis. For the purposes of valuation it would be necessary for some institutions to mark both the bond and the swap to market every day. Thus the return available from the constituent parts of the asset swap could increase or decrease relative to the packaged return. In order to avoid the administrative and financial implications of this, many asset swap buyers package the investment on a par/par basis. That is the bond is bought at par, whether it is trading at a discount or a premium, and it is redeemed at par. This structuring process is identical to that used in the creation of par/par structures in the new issue market. The par/par structure sometimes obviates the need for daily mark-to-market as it can be argued that the investment was purchased at par, will be held until maturity and will be redeemed at par.

FRNs usually enjoy much greater liquidity than the secondary market for asset swap packages. This can be a very important consideration for investors. Asset swap packages consequently have much wider bid/offer spreads than the corresponding floating-rate notes, where the latter exist. Unwinding an asset swap can be a much more expensive proposition than selling a floating-rate note.

Determining a bond price from an asset swap target

What price can an investor afford to pay for an 8% coupon 3-year bond if the investor's required return is Libor + 25 basis points? The 3-year interest rate swap price is 7.57/7.60 semi-annually, actual/360.

Question

If the investor enters into a swap paying 7.60 semi-annually on a money market basis, then it would be possible to receive 6-month Libor flat.

Answer

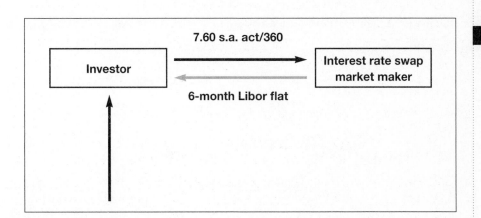

Fig 6.6

So in order to be paid 6-month Libor plus 25 basis points it is necessary for the investor to pay 7.60 plus 25 basis points or 7.85% semi-annually, actual/360 (see Figure 6.6).

Fig 6.7

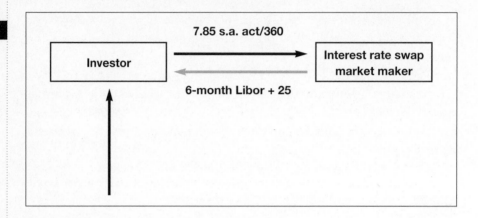

So the bond yield required to drive this transaction is 7.85% semi-annual act/360 (see Figure 6.7). The 8% 3-year bond is quoted on an annual 30/360 basis, so it is necessary to compound the semi-annual yield to its annual equivalent and to convert the day count from act/360 to 30/360. This is 8.115% per annum 30/360.

7.85% semi-annually act/360 = 8.004% per annum act/360
$$(1+(7.85/200))\wedge2$$

8.004% per annum act/360 = 8.115% per annum 30/360
$$(8.004*365/360)$$

So if the bond yield required to drive the asset swap is 8.115% per annum, 30/360 and the coupon is 8% per annum for three years, then the investor would need to be able to buy the bond at a price of 99.70%.

n	i	PV	PMT	FV
3	8.115	−99.70	8.00	100.00

Calculating the swap price given the bond yield

A 3-year 8% coupon bond, priced at par can be swapped to a floating-rate basis to generate a return of 6-month Libor + 25 basis points (see Figure 6.8).

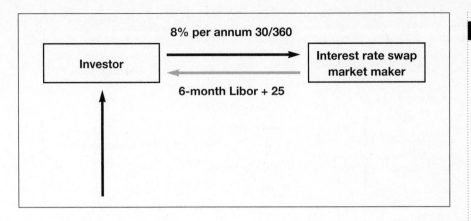

Fig 6.8

In this transaction the investor is paying 8% per annum, 30/360 to the interest rate swap market maker in return for a payment of 6-month Libor + 25 basis points. The market rate for the swap transaction is the rate which the investor would pay in order to receive a return of 6-month Libor flat.

It is necessary therefore to approximate 25 basis points semi-annual (act/360) on an annual bond basis.

s.a. act/360	p.a. act/360	p.a. 30/360
7.250	7.381	7.280
7.000	7.122	7.025

The annual differential on a bond basis is therefore approximately 25.5 basis points:

$$(7.2802 - 7.0249)$$

Subtracting 25.5 basis points from 8% p.a. 30/360 gives the swap rate which is 7.745% p.a. 30/360.

So the market rate available in the swap transaction was 7.745% per annum 30/360 and the bond yield was 8% per annum 30/360 (see Figure 6.9).

This enabled the investor to restructure the deal in order to produce a return on a floating-rate basis of 6-month Libor + 25 basis points. This was achieved by increasing the fixed-rate payment from 7.745% to 8% while simultaneously increasing the floating rate from 6-month Libor flat to 6-month Libor + 25 basis points.

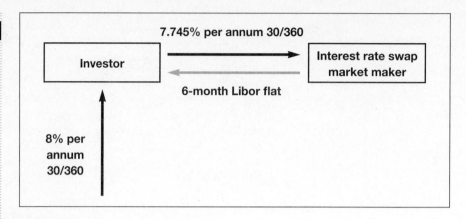

Fig 6.9

7.745% per annum 30/360

Investor → Interest rate swap market maker

6-month Libor flat

8% per annum 30/360

Question

Asset swap

An 8% 3-year bond has a price of 100.50%. If the 3-year swap rate is 7.50% per annum 30/360, what is the floating-rate return available in an asset swap package?

Answer

The yield to maturity on the bond is 7.807%:

n	i	PV	PMT	FV
3	7.807	−100.50	8.00	100.00

So the bond yield is 30.7 basis points higher than the swap rate (see Figure 6.10).

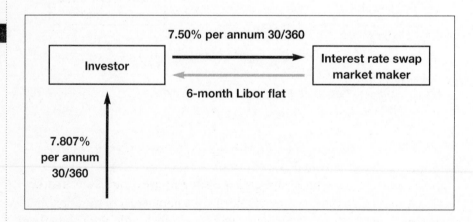

Fig 6.10

7.50% per annum 30/360

Investor → Interest rate swap market maker

6-month Libor flat

7.807% per annum 30/360

The approximate difference between the bond yield and the swap rate expressed semi-annually on a money market basis is 29 basis points:

p.a. 30/360	s.a. 30/360	s.a. act/360
7.807	7.660	7.555
7.500	7.364	7.263
0.307	0.295	0.291

So the approximate spread we could offer is 29 basis points over Libor:

$$7.555 - 7.263$$
$$= 0.291$$

A better approximation can be achieved by using the following formula. Note that this is the same formula used in calculating the borrower's all-in cost of floating-rate funds in the new issue arbitrage process.

To convert annual basis points (30/360) to a semi-annual equivalent (actual/360):

(p.a. basis points * 360/((1+(1+s.a. lending rate*182.5/360))*182.5)
(30.7 * 360/((1+(1+0.0736*182.5/360))*182.5)
= 29.7 basis points

So an arranger of such a transaction could offer an investor Libor plus 29 or 30 basis points.

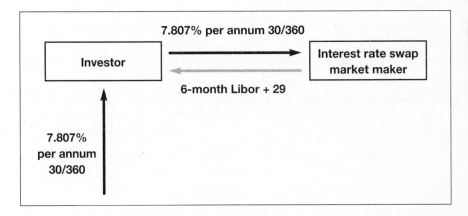

Fig 6.11

In structuring an asset swap, arrangers, or interest rate swap market makers, are often willing to enable their clients to create a par/par structure. This means that investors will buy their bonds at par whether the market price is 105% or 95%. The difference between par and the actual price of the bond is then reflected in the swap cash flows.

In the example in Figure 6.11, if the investor required a par/par structure, then the initial outlay for the bonds would be 100% rather than 100.50%. If the nominal amount of the bonds was 10,000,000, then the interest rate swap counterparty would effectively lend the difference between par and 100.50%, or 50,000 to the investor. The swap counterparty would be repaid over the life of the transaction by the investor paying not the bond yield of 7.807% or 780,700 per annum, but the full coupon of the bond, or 800,000. In this way the swap counterparty has a mismatched cash flow with a short position of 50,000 at the start of the transaction and a long position of 19,300 each year for three years. So the 19,300 per annum in additional swap receipts is effectively repayments on the loan of 50,000.

Which rate of interest or rates of interest should the interest rate swap market maker charge the investor for this loan or series of loans? If the interest rate swap market maker is willing to lend the money at the same rate of interest as the bond yield, then there is no impact on the floating-rate return available to the investor. But if the swap counterparty chooses another rate, or rates, as it almost always will, then there is an impact on the result of the swap. Most market makers would discount the bond cash flows using a zero coupon curve which reflected the bank's cost of funds and target returns on capital as well as the investor's credit quality. This is unlikely to make a difference to a bond trading at 100.50%, but the further a bond trades away from par the bigger the difference this approach makes.

Sometimes salespeople and investors are surprised at the results of an asset swap. In looking at the bond yield, it is tempting to subtract the swap rate and take this as the floating-rate yield. While this approach is fine for an approximation, or as an indication of what might be possible in an asset swap, it does not take into consideration the difference between the way cash flows are priced in a bond issue and the way swap traders price cash flows. Swap traders won't subtract the bond yield from the swap rate, they will discount the cash flows of the bond at a series of rates, reflecting a curve, rather than a maturity rate.

Rules 803.1 and 803.2

The International Securities Markets Association (ISMA) encourages conformity in the bond markets by suggesting a methodology for calculating bond yields in rule 803.1 and recommending to its members that any deviation from this methodology should be communicated at the same time as the yield is quoted (803.2). The methodology outlined in rule 803.1 is the internal rate of return. So an 8% annual coupon bond with a yield to maturity of 8% has a price of par.

So in the bond markets there is a clear convention for quoting yields using a single discount rate, the maturity rate. This is consistent with the compound interest formula and therefore has two basic assumptions: the first is that the yield curve is flat and the second is that it will not move, or if it does it will return to its current levels on coupon payment dates.

These assumptions do not necessarily interfere with an investor's use of yields to maturity to compare investments of similar maturity and price, particularly if the investor is working with bonds which are trading at or close to par.

But these assumptions play havoc with the valuation of a swap book, and so swap traders use rates which reflect the yield curve rather than the maturity rate of the cash flow. Essentially swap traders use a series of rates to value cash flows rather than one rate.

If a bond is trading at par, then the results of discounting the cash flows using a series of zero coupon rates and a single maturity rate are the same. But the further a bond trades away from par, the greater this difference becomes.

Applications of equity derivatives products

Most swap transactions involve the change of risk. From fixed to floating, for example, or from dollars to yen. Equity derivatives often involve the change of risk from an exposure to the equity markets to the money markets or *vice versa*.

A fund manager with an exposure to the S&P 500 who feels bearish about the prospects for US equities over the next 12 months could consider selling stocks and investing in the money markets. There are potentially high transaction costs associated with this. The fund manager will incur the cost of the bid offer spread on the stocks when buying them back one year from now. There could also be taxes associated with the purchase of stocks, depending on the country in question.

An equity index swap based on the S&P 500 (see Figure 6.12) could offer the fund manager a more cost-effective solution to this problem. The fund manager agrees to pay any dividends plus any gain in the underlying index to the counterparty in return for receiving a money market index, such as Libor, and any losses in the index.

Fig 6.12

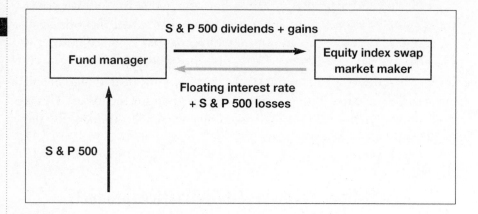

The fund manager cannot benefit from an increase in the index but will not suffer as a result of a fall in the index during the life of the index swap. So the investor's risk has been switched for the life of the deal from the equity market to the money market. At the maturity of the transaction the fund manager is in the same position as before the deal took place, that is, long of the S & P 500. It has not been necessary to sell any stock and therefore it is not necessary for the fund manager to buy any back.

In Figure 6.12, the fund manager is eliminating an exposure to the stock market, and equity risk, and exchanging it for an exposure to the money market and interest rate risk. Equity index swaps can also be used to create an exposure to the stock market and equity risk, as Figure 6.13 illustrates. In this example the investor will benefit from any upward movement in the equity index, just as if the investor owned a portfolio of investments replicating the S & P 500, and will pay away any downward movement in the index, or suffer the same losses as would an owner of the equity index itself. The investor does not actually

Fig 6.13

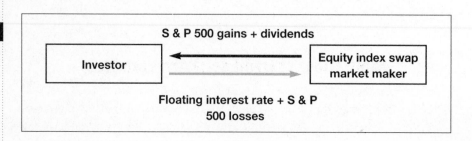

own any stock and has used the swap as a tool for changing money market risk into equity risk.

Because there is an uncertainty of the flows in an equity index swap, since neither party to the transaction knows whether the index is going to move up or down, and neither knows to what extent the index will move up or down, there is considerable potential credit exposure in these transactions. Sometimes market makers and their clients agree to collateralize these transactions, that is, they mark the deal to market and ensure that the party who is losing money is good for the losses. This is very similar to the process used in exchange-traded products for the calculation of variation margin.

Applications of commodity derivatives products

Commodity swaps allow traders and hedgers to eliminate their exposure to a commodity risk while simultaneously creating an exposure in the money market. Alternatively, as is the case with equity index swaps, they can be used as a way of creating an exposure to commodity risk without actually buying the underlying commodity itself. The effect of this is to change the hedger's or trader's exposure from commodity to money market risk or *vice versa*.

A gold producer, for example, has a revenue stream which depends upon the value of the gold sold in the marketplace. As the gold price rises, so the producer's revenue increases. If the gold producer wants to fix its return for a given period, then a commodity swap provides it with one means of achieving this. The gold producer contracts to receive a fixed price for a given quantity of gold over a given maturity and agrees in return to pay a floating interest rate. The gold producer will now no longer benefit from a rise in the gold price, but will no longer suffer from its fall. Thus the producer has effectively switched its risk from the gold price to the money market. In essence then, commodity swaps follow the pattern of interest rate, currency and equity swaps in that they allow payers and receivers to change their risk from one market to another.

Applications of credit derivatives products

Credit derivatives are a relative newcomer to the world of swaps, although some practitioners argue that the transfer of credit risk by the issuance of letters of credit makes them considerably older. In their current form, credit derivatives emerged in 1990 when structured notes were issued which allowed banks with large exposures to Japanese banks to free up their lines to the Japanese financial sector.

Credit derivatives are however fundamentally different from interest rate, currency, equity and commodity derivatives in that the financial structure of these products is more or less the same. All interest rate swaps are fundamentally alike although there are many structural variations available to meet customers' requirements. The same is true for currency, commodity and equity swaps. But credit derivatives have more than one type. There is more than one way to divide the structures but here is one possible split:

- Credit default swaps
- Total rate of return swaps
- Credit forwards.

Credit default swaps

In a credit default swap, one party receives a fee in return for agreeing to pay its counterparty any credit loss resulting from default by a given borrower on an agreed principal amount. For example, a bank may agree to pay any credit losses associated with US$ 1,000,000,000 Mexican government debt over a period of two years in return for a fee of 0.05% per annum on the principal amount.

The deal is consistent with other derivatives in that it enables a bank to change its credit exposure to Mexico and therefore the bank has changed its risk. All derivatives do this. But this structure is like an insurance contract in that one party is paying premiums to the other against the promise of a payment if the borrower defaults. So credit derivatives differ from other derivatives in that there is a greater variety of structures available. All credit derivatives are not fundamentally the same.

Total rate of return swaps

Total rate of return swaps are the credit derivative structure which most closely resembles interest rate, currency, equity and commodity swaps. In fact total rate of return swaps are very similar in structure to equity index swaps. In an equity index swap, the equity buyer receives dividends plus any improvement in the underlying index. The equity buyer pays any fall in the underlying index to the equity seller.

> Equity buyer receives dividends plus any improvement in the underlying index.

In a total rate of return swap the credit buyer receives interest income on the underlying credit plus any improvement on the underlying credit. The credit buyer pays any deterioration in the underlying credit to the seller.

> Credit buyer receives interest income on the underlying credit plus any improvement on the underlying credit.

Credit forwards

Credit forwards are like a forward market in bond spreads. If the absolute yield on a bond, or its yield to maturity, is benchmarked against a government curve, then the bond's credit spread is isolated. For example, if a bond issued by Coca-Cola yields 5.80% and the government bond of an equivalent maturity is 5.50%, then it can be said that the Coca-Cola bond is trading at a spread of 30 basis points (0.30%) over the government curve. An investor buying this bond receives 5.50% because of the currency and the maturity and 0.30% because the bond is issued by Coca-Cola. So Coca-Cola's credit spread is 30 basis points.

If Coca-Cola's credit improved, then its bonds would yield less, that is, the borrower would pay less for a new bond issue and investors receive less in yield for buying Coca-Cola's bonds. Coca-Cola's credit spread has narrowed or tightened. If the yield on the bonds fell to 5.70% then the borrower's spread has tightened from 30 basis points to 20 basis points. If, on the other hand, Coca-Cola's credit deteriorated, then its spread would widen, that is, the borrower would pay more for a new issue and investors would receive more in return for accepting the borrowers credit.

While it is generally true to say that a borrower's credit spread will narrow if the borrower's credit improves, and will widen if the borrower's credit deteriorates, this does not tell the whole story.

> A borrower's credit spread will narrow if the borrower's credit improves.

A borrower's credit spread is not an absolute measure of credit risk: it is not possible, for example, to produce a formula which will calculate credit spreads for borrowers whose financial data meets certain criteria. The credit spread is a measure of the relative demand for a borrower's credit.

> **The credit spread is a measure of the relative demand for a borrower's credit.**

So the credit spread reflects the market price for a borrower's credit which is a function of both the borrower's credit quality and the current level of demand in the marketplace for this particular borrower's debt.

Credit forwards allow banks and their clients to trade a borrower's credit. For example, a bank could buy a particular credit at a strike price of 35 basis points over the government curve for one year in one year's time. Having agreed on a principal amount and a method of referencing or calculating the credit spread one year from now, the two parties would settle up, based on the change in the price of the borrower's credit.

For example, if the spread widens to 55 basis points in one year's time then the buyer of the credit forward would have incurred a loss. The buyer had a long position in the credit and the value of the credit has fallen. Hence the loss. So the credit buyer pays the credit seller 20 basis points on the principal amount on which the two parties had dealt.

If, on the other hand, the credit spread narrowed to 25 basis points then the credit buyer has made a gain and the credit seller a loss. The credit buyer was long the underlying which has improved in price, hence its gain. The seller was short of a commodity which has gone up in value, hence its loss.

Credit derivatives and credit arbitrage

So credit forwards enable banks and their clients to buy and sell credit risk in a forward market. One of the significant aspects of this from a loan and capital markets perspective is that it provides another way for parties to sell credit. In itself, this is not significant but the credit arbitrage which exists between the bond and the syndicated loans market exists because the markets are inefficient. One of the contributors to an efficient market is the ability to go short. Indeed, for a market to work well, and for arbitrage opportunities to become scarcer, it is a requirement that participants can create short as well as long positions. If a bank or a trader believes a credit is cheap, then it can buy the underlying credit which will tend to push the price up. Equally, if a bank or a trader believes a credit to be expensive or overpriced, then credit forwards provide one means for expressing this view.

Credit derivatives are also used by commercial banks to change the credit exposure on their loan books. In the past, lending and credit risk were inseparable: a bank making a loan to a company took the company's credit risk on to its book until the loan was repaid. This is analogous to funding and interest rate swaps.

In the same way that banks use interest rate swaps to separate funding and interest rate risk, banks use credit derivatives to separate lending and credit risk. If a bank's credit line to a borrower or a country is full, or if its appetite for a certain credit has been satisfied, it can continue to lend to the borrower, but reduce the bank's credit exposure by selling the underlying credit to a counterparty which wants to buy the name. A bank with good relationships with the property sector which believes that the firm has a large enough credit exposure to justify turning away prospective business could consider writing more business but selling the credit risk. The bank would earn the difference between the margin charged to the borrower and the cost of selling the credit risk.

Managing a Swap Book

Overview

This chapter examines the major issues involved in running a swaps book. It starts by looking at the mark-to-market process for both fixed and floating cash flows before exploring some of the portfolio management issues relating to running a book. It looks at the relationship between fixed-rate agreements (FRAs), futures and swaps and at how they can be used as hedging tools. The chapter ends by illustrating these techniques applied to two particular cases: amortizing swaps and reverse floating-rate notes (FRNs).

The first component of managing a swap book is the ability to mark an individual swap to market.

Marking to market

Marking a long position (a purchase) to market requires the valuing of the position at current market rates.

> **Marking to market means establishing the net value of a position.**

If a commodity has been purchased, it is necessary to establish what the net position would be if a sale were made. The owner of a house purchased for US$ 500,000 could mark this asset to market by calculating the net value of the position if a sale was made. If the current market price of the house is US$ 600,000, then the mark-to-market value of the position would be US$ 100,000:

$$+US\$\ 600,000 - US\$\ 500,000$$

If the value of the house was now US$ 450,000, then the position would have a mark-to-market loss of US$ 50,000:

$$+US\$\ 450,000 - US\$\ 500,000$$

In the first instance, where the value of the house is US$ 600,000, the position can be described as "in-the-money" or profitable. The profit has not been realized however and could therefore become larger or disappear subject to changes in market rates.

> **Mark-to-market values represent unrealized gains and losses.**

Marking a short position (a sale) to market involves establishing the net value of a position if the short is covered, that is, if a purchase were to be made. This is a more difficult concept than covering long positions but is identical in its application. It involves the hypothetical reversing of the original position in order to establish a net value of the position.

> **Marking to market is the hypothetical reversing of a position in order to establish its net value.**

A trader sells one BP share to a client at £8.50 for delivery in 7 days' time. Before leaving for the day, the trader marks this position to market by comparing it with the current market price. If the market price is £9.50, the trader has a mark-to-market loss of £1.00. If the market price is £8.00, the trader has a mark-to-market gain of 50p.

Marking swaps to market

Swaps are symmetrical risk instruments. This has the following implications:

- It is neither better nor worse to be a payer or a receiver in a swap transaction. A view on interest rates is simply a matter of opinion and will not usually guarantee a profit.
- There are no fees or charges payable from either party to its counterparty.
- Neither party is required to reward its counterparty for entering into a swap transaction.
- Neither party has a greater chance of profiting from a transaction.
- The profit from a market move in one direction is equal to the loss for the same move in the other direction.
- The net value of a trade, at the time a deal is struck, is approximately equal to zero: it is in fact equal to the market maker's bid/offer spread.
- The approximate mark-to-market value of a symmetrical risk instrument at the time a deal is struck is zero. So marking a swap to market essentially involves determining the extent to which the price at which a trade took place differs from the current market price.

Marking the fixed cash flows of a swap to market

It is sometimes said that the valuation of swaps is like the valuation of bonds. An interest rate swap, it could be argued, is like being long, or short, of a fixed-rate bond and short, or long, of a floating-rate note. In the example shown in Figure 7.1, a trader has transacted a swap in which a fixed rate of interest, 4.25% per annum, will be paid to the trader by a counterparty and, in return, the trader has contracted to pay a floating rate of interest, 6-month D-mark Libor.

Fig 7.1

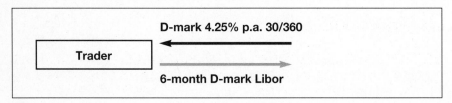

Is this like being long a fixed-rate bond and short a floating-rate note? Some market participants say that it is. Will the fixed-rate cash flows behave like those in a fixed-rate bond? Is their sensitivity to interest rate risk equal to those of a fixed-rate bond?

Some would argue that the fixed-rate cash flows in the swap have fundamental differences from those of a fixed-rate bond:

> **An interest rate swap has no redemption amount. It is quite usual to value a bond using a single discount rate.**

When valuing the cash flows in the fixed leg of a swap, it is necessary to use a series of discount rates reflecting values which could be realized without any residual reinvestment risk.

There are three widely used valuation techniques for determining the present value of a series of cash flows:

- A maturity rate
- A series of forward/forward rates
- A series of zero coupon rates.

When a swap is valued, it is usual to use a series of zero coupon rates rather than a maturity rate. Zero coupon rates always break even to a series of forward/forward rates. It is much easier however, in a database or a spreadsheet to use zero coupon rates rather than forward/forwards. If, for example, a 50-year swap was valued using forward/forward rates it would be discounted back at a different forward rate for each day of its life. This involves discounting the cash flow at about 18,000 different rates. It is clearly an easier process, even with the use of technology to discount the cash flow back from 50 years to its present value using a single zero coupon rate which is the weighted average of the 18,000 forward/forward rates.

Hedging fixed rates

Hedging fixed-rate positions involves an appreciation of the differences between hedging bond positions and swap positions.

Hedging bond positions

If a trader makes or loses 1% per annum on a position, then the resultant profit or loss is sensitive to the maturity of the position taken. Here are three examples:

- overnight depo trader makes 1%
- money market trader makes 1% on a 6-month position
- bond trader makes 1% on a 5-year position.

In order to quantify the profit on these trades it is necessary to establish whether the gains are **"flat"** or whether they are **annual.** For example, overnight depo rates are quoted in terms of the annual rate, so a change in the value of an overnight position by 1% is worth approximately 1/360 of this amount. So in **gross** terms, without reflecting the amounts in terms of their **present values**, a trader with a 1% change in a 1-year position has a gain or a loss of 360 times as much. While the **nominal** amounts are equal the **effective** amounts differ significantly.

In a position which runs for more than one year, the difference is even more significant. A trader making a nominal gain of 1% in a 5-year position makes a gross gain of 1% each year for five years, or 5%. It is **market practice** to **discount** this to its **present value.** When one basis point per annum is discounted to its present value it is known as "the PV of an 01" or **PV01.** In cash terms it is often referred to as "the dollar value of an 01," "the DV of an 01" or simply **DV01.**

In calculating the PV01 a trader or risk manager is determining the **rate** at which money is gained or lost. This is the **sensitivity** of the position to changes in market prices (or yields).

When **traders** and **risk managers hedge** their positions, sensitivity to risk is often determined so that a correlation between the underlying position and the hedge position can be calculated. The idea in a hedge is to make money in one position at the same rate as it is being lost in the other. **Sensitivity** is an effective way of estimating this.

Modified duration is frequently used as a tool in the calculation of a **bond's sensitivity.** The modified duration of a 4% annual coupon 3-year bond with a yield to maturity of 8% is 2.666:

Years	Bond flows	Discount	PV	Weighted PV
1	4.000	0.926	3.704	3.704
2	4.000	0.857	3.429	6.859
3	104.000	0.794	82.559	247.676
			89.692	258.238
yield	0.08		**Macaulay**	**2.879**
coupon	4		**Modified**	**2.666**

Modified duration is calculated by dividing Macaulay's duration by 1 plus the bond's yield divided by the number of coupons per annum:

$$\text{Modified D} = \text{Macaulay}/1 + \text{ytm}/n$$

where *ytm* is the yield to maturity expressed as a decimal, and *n* is the number of coupons paid each year (in this example, 2.879/1.08).

So the modified duration is 2.666.

Macaulay's duration is 2.879 and is calculated by weighting the present value of each of the bond's cash flows (i.e., the bond's price) by their maturity and dividing the sum of these by the bond's price.

Question

Calculate Macaulay's duration and modify it, for a 3-year 16% bond which yields 8% per annum to its maturity.

Answer

Years	Bond flows	Discount	PV	Weighted PV
1	16.000	0.926	14.815	14.815
2	16.000	0.857	13.717	27.435
3	116.000	0.794	92.085	276.254
			120.617	318.503
yield	0.08		**Macaulay**	**2.641**
coupon	16		**Modified**	**2.445**

Questions

1. A trader has paid US$ 12,062,000 for 10 million 16% 3 years. What is the sensitivity of this position to a change in yield of 1% per annum?

2. What is the PV01 of this position?

Answers

1. In order to establish the sensitivity of the position to a change in yield of 1%, calculate the bond's price at yields of 7% and 9%. At a yield of 7% per annum the bond has a price of 123.62%.

Years	Bond flows	Discount	PV	Weighted PV
1	16.000	0.935	14.953	14.953
2	16.000	0.873	13.975	27.950
3	116.000	0.816	94.691	284.072
			123.619	326.975
yield	0.07		**Macaulay**	**2.645**
coupon	16		**Modified**	**2.472**

At a yield of 9% the bond has a price of 117.72%.

Years	Bond flows	Discount	PV	Weighted PV
1	16.000	0.917	14.679	14.679
2	16.000	0.842	13.467	26.934
3	116.000	0.772	89.573	268.720
			117.719	310.333
yield	0.09		**Macaulay**	**2.636**
coupon	16		**Modified**	**2.419**

It is now possible to calculate the sensitivity of the position to a 1% change in yield.

12,062,000.00	12,362,000.00
11,772,000.00	12,062,000.00
290,000.00	300,000.00

It is possible to approximate the sensitivity of a position to a change in yield by multiplying the change in yield by the dirty price of the bond and its modified duration:

Years	Bond flows	Discount	PV	Weighted PV
1	16.000	0.926	14.815	14.815
2	16.000	0.857	13.717	27.435
3	116.000	0.794	92.085	276.254
			120.617	318.503
yield	0.08		**Macaulay**	**2.641**
coupon	16		**Modified**	**2.445**

$$10,000,000 * 120.62\% * 1\% * 2.445$$
$$= 294,915.90$$

2. The PV01 is therefore 2,949.16

or

$$10,000,000 * 120.62\% * 0.01\% * 2.445$$
$$= 2,949.16$$

Question How many 5% 3-year bonds, yielding 8%, would the trader need to sell to balance the risk (i.e., what is his hedge position)?

Years	Bond flows	Discount	PV	Weighted PV
1	5.000	0.926	4.630	4.630
2	5.000	0.857	4.287	8.573
3	105.000	0.794	<u>83.352</u>	<u>250.057</u>
			92.269	263.260
yield	0.08		**Macaulay**	**2.853**
coupon	5		**Modified**	**2.642**

The trader needs a position which will move at the same rate, or has the same sensitivity to risk. If the trader thinks there is a correlation of one between the two bonds then the change in value of the hedge bond (5% coupon) needs to be 2,949.16 for a one basis point change in yield.

$$\text{Hedge position} * 92.27\% * 0.01\% * 2.642$$
$$= 2,949.16$$

Therefore his hedge position is:

$$= 2,949.16/92.27\% * 0.01\% * 2.642$$
$$= 12,097,761.02$$

Hedging swaps

The perfect hedge for a swap is another swap which mirrors the payments of the first transaction. When this is not available, there are a number of alternatives. The most commonly used is to cover the position, short term, by taking a position in a government market either by buying government bonds themselves or by using government bond futures. A payer of the fixed rate in a swap will buy government bonds, or futures, to produce fixed-rate income (generating the cash to buy the bonds by borrowing floating-rate funds which would hedge the floating-rate position).

One of the problems with this approach is that it will only earn the government yield from the bond purchase while it is necessary to pay governments plus a spread in the swap transaction. The maturities, yields and coupons of the swap and of government bonds are also different. Where a government bond futures market exists, this can provide a very attractive alternative to buying government bonds themselves. The hedger will incur the bid/offer spread in the government bond market or the futures market when liquidating the hedge. This will become necessary when a matching swap has been found for the original transaction. The bid offer spread in futures is often significantly less than it is the underlying cash market.

An alternative would be to match the swap position by offsetting a transaction with a different maturity. This requires some finetuning as a position of 25 million in two years clearly does not hedge a position of 25 million in five years. In order to balance such a transaction it is necessary to ensure that the present value of the two cash flows from the two swap transactions is equal: if the 2-year and 5-year swap rates are 10% p.a. 30/360 and 11% p.a. 30/360 respectively, what is the approximate size of position required to cover 25,000,000 for two years?

Maturity	Cash flow	Discount rate	Present value
2 years	10.00	10.00	17.36
5 years	11.00	11.00	40.65

The present values are calculated as follows, bearing in mind that there is no exchange of principal at maturity in an interest rate swap. The objective in this calculation is to ensure that the present values of the two cash flows is equal at the time the hedge is put in place.

The swap rate for two years of 10% is discounted at 10% for two years. This gives a present value of 17.355%. This makes sense as the gross value of the two flows is 20%.

n	i	PV	PMT	FV
2	10	17.355	10.00	0.00

The 5-year swap rate of 11%, worth 55% gross, has a present value of 40.655% when discounted at 11%. Strictly speaking these two cash flows should be discounted using a zero coupon curve, but here an approximation will suffice as it is not possible to hedge precisely using this method. A bookrunner offsetting one swap with another is changing the book's risk from the absolute direction of movements in rates to a play on the direction of changes in the shape of the yield curve.

n	i	PV	PMT	FV
5	11	40.655	11.00	0.00

These present values show the relative size of the 2-and 5-year positions. On a simple, non-compounded basis, a 5-year position is two and a half times the size of a position in the five years. This does not reflect the time value of money or the yield differential between two and five years. These can be reflected by discounting a 2- and a 5-year position to their respective present values discounted at the 2- and 5-year rates. If the 5-year present value is divided by the 2-year present value the relative risk in a 5- and a 2-year position is established:

$$40.655/17.355 = 2.343$$

So the approximate profit or loss in a 5-year position for similar moves in interest rates is about 2.343 times more than in a 2-year position. Hedging 25 million two years would require a 5-year position of about 10 million:

$$25 \text{ million}/2.343 = 10.67 \text{ million}$$

or

$$25 \text{ million} * 17.355/40.655$$
$$= 10.672 \text{ million}$$

While it is more accurate to use a zero coupon curve to value these cash flows, a swap trader using this technique as a way of estimating the yield curve risk in a swap book is not likely to be looking for an exact hedge. It is much more likely that a trader would consider where the largest gaps in the book are and use standard maturity swaps as a way of reducing the firm's yield curve exposure. It is also important to realize that this relationship changes as interest rates move so this does not represent a perfect hedge.

It is also possible to calculate the size of the required position in cash terms. A 2-year swap at 10% per annum 30/360 on 25 million produces two fixed-rate cash flows of 2,500,000 which can be expressed as a present value of 4,338,842.98:

n	i	PV	PMT	FV
2	10	4,338,842.98	2,500,000.00	0.00

Having established the present value of the 2-year position it is necessary to calculate what swap payment in five years at 11% has the same present value:

n	i	PV	PMT	FV
5	11	4,338,842.98	1,173,962.09	0.00

The interest payment in the five years is 1,173,962.09. What is the notional principal amount which at an interest rate of 11% results in this payment?

$$\text{Notional} * 11/100 = 1{,}173{,}962.09$$
$$\text{Notional} * 0.11 = 1{,}173{,}962.09$$
$$\text{Dividing both sides by } 0.11:$$
$$\text{Notional} = 1{,}173{,}962.09/0.11$$
$$\text{Notional} = 10.672 \text{ million}$$

Hedging a portfolio of swaps with a single swap

Here are the three transactions which constitute a book of swaps. The bookrunner has an opportunity to lay off some of the risk resulting from these transactions in a single 5-year swap transaction at a rate of 11.30% per annum 30/360. What amount of five years would balance the trader's book?

2 years 10.75% p.a. 30/360 on 25 million
4 years 11.25% p.a. 30/360 on 30 million
7 years 11.50% p.a. 30/360 on 10 million

The trader was a payer in the 2- and 4-year transactions and a receiver in the 7-year transaction.

First calculate the present value of the fixed-rate cash flows, discounted at the swap rates. The 2-year swap is 10.75% per annum, so discounting this rate at 10.75%:

- 2-year PV is 18.471 (10.75@10.75)

n	i	PV	PMT	FV
2	10.75	18.471	10.75	0.00

- 4-year PV is 34.717 (11.25@11.25)

n	i	PV	PMT	FV
4	11.25	34.717	11.25	0.00

■ 5-year PV is 41.450(11.30@11.30)

n	i	PV	PMT	FV
5	11.3	41.450	11.30	0.00

■ 7-year PV is 53.326 (11.50@11.50)

n	i	PV	PMT	FV
7	11.5	53.326	11.50	0.00

These figures show the present values of the coupon payments in the swaps expressed as percentages. In order to establish the cash value of each position it is necessary to multiply each of the present value factors by the notional principal amount of the transactions:

$$25 \text{ million} * 18.471\% = 4,617,750$$
$$30 \text{ million} * 34.717\% = 10,415,100$$
$$10 \text{ million} * 53.326\% = 5,332,600$$

The total of the payments in present value terms is 15,032,850:

$$4,617,750 + 10,415,100$$
$$= 15,032,850$$

Subtracting the present value of the 7-year receipts shows the net position:

$$15,032,850 - 5,332,600$$
$$= 9,700,250$$

The hedge amount is the notional principal amount which has a present value of 9,700,250 at a discount rate of the 5-year swap rate of 11.30% per annum 30/360:

n	i	PV	PMT	FV
5	11.3	9,700,250.00	–2,644,435.58	0.00

Dividing the interest amount by the interest rate gives the principal amount:

$$2,644,435.58/0.113$$
$$= 23,402,084.81$$

So about 25 million five years will give the trader a better balanced swap book.

It is possible to calculate the approximate balancing amount by converting the notional principal amounts of the three existing transactions to their 5-year equivalent amounts. The 2- and 4-year 5-year equivalents, less the 7-year 5-year equivalent are 23.4 million:

$$25 \text{ million} * 18.471/41.450 = 11.14 \text{ million}$$
$$30 \text{ million} * 34.717/41.450 = 25.13 \text{ million}$$
$$10 \text{ million} * 53.326/41.450 = 12.87 \text{ million}$$

$$11.14 \text{ million} + 25.13 \text{ million} - 12.87 \text{ million} = 23.40 \text{ million}$$

A 5-year swap on 23,400,000 as a receiver of fixed interest, a payer of floating results in the following fixed-rate cash flows and present value amounts:

Years	2 years	4 years	5 years	7 years
1	-2,687,500.00	-3,375,000.00	2,644,200.00	1,150,000.00
2	-2,687,500.00	-3,375,000.00	2,644,200.00	1,150,000.00
3		-3,375,000.00	2,644,200.00	1,150,000.00
4		-3,375,000.00	2,644,200.00	1,150,000.00
5			2,644,200.00	1,150,000.00
6				1,150,000.00
7				1,150,000.00
	PV @ 10.75	@ 11.25	@ 11.30	@ 11.50
	-4,617,730.00	-10,415,108.00	9,699,386.00	5,332,590.00

The present value of the receipts is approximately equal to the present value of the payments. This is a methodology which is often the first step in calculating the net risk between two positions.

After executing the 5-year swap, rates move up by 10 basis points across the yield curve. The swap trader's salesforce are successful in creating matches for each of the four original swaps.

	Swap rate
2 years	10.85
4 years	11.35
5 years	11.40
7 years	11.60

The trader receives fixed rates of 10.85 and 11.35 respectively in the new 2- and 4-year swaps and pays fixed rates of 11.40 and 11.60 respectively in the new 5- and 7-year deals. There are therefore now eight swaps on the trader's book: two matching deals in each maturity. What is the swap trader's net cash flow for Years 1 to 7 and what is the net present value of the book?

Calculating the trader's net position

The following four cash flows represent a 10 basis point change in each of our transactions. The fifth column shows net cash flows. The figures at the bottom of each column show the present value of each swap transaction discounted at the current swap rates. A zero curve would give a more precise answer, but here the swap rates have been used as an approximation.

2 years	4 years	7 years	5 years	Net
25,000.00	30,000.00	−10,000.00	−23,400.00	21,600.00
25,000.00	30,000.00	−10,000.00	−23,400.00	21,600.00
	30,000.00	−10,000.00	−23,400.00	−3,400.00
	30,000.00	−10,000.00	−23,400.00	−3,400.00
		−10,000.00	−23,400.00	−33,400.00
		−10,000.00		−10,000.00
		−10,000.00		−10,000.00
@ 10.85	@ 11.35	@ 11.60	@ 11.40	
42,899.00	92,382.00	−46,222.00	−85,620.00	3,439.00

$$42,899 + 92,382 - 46,222 - 85,620$$
$$= 135,281 - 131,842$$
$$= 3,439$$

This values each of the swap cash flows at the swap rate for its maturity. The net cash flows from the 2-year swap are valued at the 2-year rate, the net cash flows from the 4-year swap are valued at the 4-year rate, the net cash flows from the 5-year swap are valued at the 5-year rate and the net cash flows from the 7-year swap are valued at the 7-year rate.

If the net cash flow is discounted at the 7-year swap rate, the present value is 2,951.21.

In order to obtain a consistent value, whether valuing the net cash flows from each pair of swaps or valuing the net cash flows of the book as a whole market makers use a zero coupon curve. The difference in our two methods here is insignificant but it increases as the swap book becomes larger, as the mismatched positions become greater and as the yield curve steepens.

Net	Net PV @ 11.6%
21,600.00	19,354.84
21,600.00	17,343.05
−3,400.00	−2,446.17
−3,400.00	−2,191.91
−33,400.00	−19,294.14
−10,000.00	−5,176.25
−10,000.00	−4,638.21
	2,951.21

In addition to measuring the value of the swap book in present value terms it is possible to determine the internal rate of return of the book.

f	CLx
21,600.00	STO 1
	STO 2
3,400.00	CHS STO 3
	STO 4
33,400.00	CHS STO 5
10,000.00	CHS STO 6
	STO 7
7	n
f	IRR

The internal rate of return of the net cash flow is 9.135%. This means that if the first two cash flows are invested at 9.135% throughout the term of the book then the subsequent cash flows can be paid exactly from the proceeds of the investment and at Year 7 there will be precisely 10,000 remaining to meet the last payment of 10,000. The target breakeven investment rate is below current market rates because the net present value of the cash flow is positive.

Having established the internal rate of return of the book, a trader can calculate the sensitivity of the book to a change in rates. Since the net present value of the cash flow is zero at the internal rate of return, the cash flow will have a positive value at a discount rate one basis point higher than the internal rate of return and a negative present value at a discount rate one basis point below the internal rate of return. Subtract one basis point from the internal rate of return calculated above and then recalculate the present value of the cash flow. The sensitivity is 13.08. For each basis point move in rates the trader will make or lose 13.08.

f	CLx
21,600.00	STO 1
	STO 2
3,400.00	CHS STO 3
	STO 4
33,400.00	CHS STO 5
10,000.00	CHS STO 6
	STO 7
7	n
f	IRR
	9.135449183
0.01	–
i	f
NPV	

Offsetting one swap with another of different maturity

EXAMPLE

Issuer	The Mortgage Bank
Amount	200,000,000.00
Maturity	7 years
Coupon	9¼%
Issue price	100.75
Amortization	Bullet
Call option	None
Listing	Luxembourg
Denominations	5,000, 50,000
Commissions	1⅞%
Expenses	60,000.00
Swap	Into floating (against 6-month Libor Act/360)
Negative pledge	Yes
Cross default	Yes
Pari passu	Yes

Market comment: The pricing of the deal at about 41 basis points over the government curve at launch was generally considered fair, if a little on the bullish side. The Mortgage Bank said it received more aggressive bids on the deal, but not on the swap. The deal, which had been priced about in line with a recent 7-year, should move in time, dealers said, but was held back by investors picking up bonds at spreads of 41 to 44 points over the curve amid some heavily discounted selling of the issue.

Question

What is the borrower's post swap floating-rate cost of funds if the 7-year swap rate is 75/70 and the government yield is 9.37 semi-annually?

Answer

In order to calculate the borrower's post swap cost of floating-rate funds it is necessary to determine the difference between the borrower's fixed-rate cost of borrowing and the swap rate and express this difference on a semi-annual act/360 basis.

The borrower's all-in cost of funds is 9.483 p.a. 30/360:

0	−197,690,000.00
1	18,500,000.00
2	18,500,000.00
3	18,500,000.00
4	18,500,000.00
5	18,500,000.00
6	18,500,000.00
7	18,500,000.00
7	200,000,000.00

The borrower would be a receiver of the fixed rate in the swap transaction at 70 over the government bond curve:

$$9.37 + 0.70$$
$$= 10.07 \text{ semi-annually}$$
$$= 10.324 \text{ p.a. } (30/360)$$

If the borrower chose to transact at this rate The Mortgage Bank would receive 20,648,000.00 and pay 6-month Libor flat:

$$200,000,000 * 10.324\%$$
$$= 20,648,000$$

The borrower might elect however to receive the internal rate of return and thus reduce both the fixed and the floating elements of the deal. This would entitle it to receive on the fixed side as follows:

$$9.483\% * 200,000,000$$
$$= 18,966,000$$

The fixed cash flow has been reduced from 10.323 to 9.483 or by 84 basis points per annum 30/360 and therefore the floating cash flow should have a similar adjustment of 80 basis points.

To convert annual basis points (30/360) to a semi-annual equivalent (actual/360):

(p.a. basis points * 360/((1+(1+s.a. lending rate*182.5/360))*182.5)
(84 * 360/((1+(1+0.107*182.5/360))*182.5)
= 80.66 s.a. act/360

The Mortgage Bank's net annual fixed-rate cash flow is now +466,000:

−18,500,000 coupon payments
+18,966,000 swap receipts

The issuer could ask to have the net annual surplus 466,000 discounted to its present value and paid "up-front," i.e., at the beginning of the transaction as an initial payment and if the borrower's all-in cost of funds is used as a discount rate the payment would be 2,307,823.12:

1	466,000.00	425,636.86
2	466,000.00	388,769.82
3	466,000.00	355,096.06
4	466,000.00	324,338.99
5	466,000.00	296,245.98
6	466,000.00	270,586.29
7	466,000.00	247,149.13
		2,307,823.12

This enables The Mortgage Bank to match its cash flow. It receives 200,000,000 at the start of the deal, pays 6-month Libor minus 80 basis points on 200,000,000 and repays 200,000,000 at maturity.

Question

The swap counterparty which dealt with The Mortgage Bank wants to hedge this transaction but is unable to find a suitable 7-year transaction. How much would the bank need to transact in the five years? 5-year governments are 9.31 semi-annually and the swap spread is 65/60. The trader treats the first transaction as being at government's plus 70 basis points against 6-month Libor flat.

Answer

The bank would be a receiver at 9.31% + 0.60% semi-annually which is equivalent to 10.156% per annum. Discounting these cash flows at 10.156 produces a present value of 38.346%:

n	i	PV	PMT	FV
5	10.156	−38.346	10.156	0.00

Repeating this process for seven years where the rate is 10.324% produces a present value of 49.727. These present value factors can now be used to calculate the approximate balancing amount in the 7-year trade:

n	i	PV	PMT	FV
7	10.324	49.730	10.324	0.00

$$200,000,000*49.730/38.346$$
$$= 259,374,488 \text{ or approximately } 260,000,000$$

Question

Interest rates move up by 20 basis points and the 5- and 7-year government yields become 9.51 semi-annually and 9.57 semi-annually. Swap spreads remain unchanged at 65/60 and 75/70. A customer pays the trader governments + 75 on 200 million seven years and the trader therefore decides to reverse the 5-year position at governments plus 65. What is the present value of the profit/loss on the four transactions? Calculate the net cash flow for each year and then calculate their net present value.

Answer

Rates move up by 20 basis points:

	5 years	7 years
governments	9.51 s.a.	9.57 s.a.
spread	60/65 s.a.	70/75 s.a.

In the original positions the trader paid 10.324% on 200,000,000 seven years and received 10.156% on 260,000,000 five years.

In the two new transactions the trader receives governments plus 75 on 200 million seven years and pays governments plus 65 on 260,000,000 five years.

G + 75 = 9.57 + 0.75 = 10.32% semi-annually which is equivalent to 10.586% per annum.

G + 65 in the five years is 9.51 plus 0.65, which is 10.16% semi-annually or 10.418% per annum.

The trader has four deals at the following rates:

$$g + 70 = 10.324\%$$
$$g + 60 = 10.156\%$$
$$g + 75 = 10.586\%$$
$$g + 65 = 10.418\%$$

The payments are:

10.324% on 200,000,000 seven years
10.418% on 260,000,000 five years

or

−20,648,000
−27,086,800

The receipts are:

10.586% on 200,000,000 seven years
10.156% on 260,000,000 five years

or

21,172,000
26,405,600

7 years	7 years	5 years	5 years	Net position
−20,648,000.00	21,172,000.00	26,405,600.00	−27,086,800.00	−157,200.00
−20,648,000.00	21,172,000.00	26,405,600.00	−27,086,800.00	−157,200.00
−20,648,000.00	21,172,000.00	26,405,600.00	−27,086,800.00	−157,200.00
−20,648,000.00	21,172,000.00	26,405,600.00	−27,086,800.00	−157,200.00
−20,648,000.00	21,172,000.00	26,405,600.00	−27,086,800.00	−157,200.00
−20,648,000.00	21,172,000.00			524,000.00
−20,648,000.00	21,172,000.00			524,000.00

At a discount rate of 10.586%, the 7-year swap rate, the net present value of the cash flow is −41,515.21. So this technique does not hedge swaps precisely but allows traders to take a view on the swap curve.

Amortizing swaps

In an amortizing swap transaction the customer often has existing debt which has an amortization schedule, the loan is gradually paid off during its life. Most international bond issues are arranged on a bullet basis, so there is a single repayment of principal at maturity. When there is a single repayment of principal at maturity, the amount of debt outstanding remains constant throughout the life of the loan. This means that when a borrower arranges a swap transaction it is a simple matter to match the amounts of the loan, or bond issue, and the swap, as neither vary during the life of the transaction. When the loan has an amortization schedule, it is necessary for the borrower to transact an amortizing swap so that as the amount of the loan decreases so the amount of the swap decreases. In the following example, the borrower wants to match an amortization schedule in a bond issue with an amortization in the swap so that on a fully hedged basis the borrower will have switched from fixed-rate debt to floating-rate debt.

CASE STUDY

ASIAN ELECTRIC POWER COMPANY

Amount	150,000,000.00
Maturity	5 years
Coupon	9¾%
Issue price	101⅝%
Call option	None
Listing	Luxembourg
Denominations	5,000.00
Commissions	1⅞%
Expenses	125,000.00
Swap	to 6-month Libor
Amortization	2-year grace period, then equal annual payments
Negative pledge	Yes
Cross default	Yes
Pari passu	Yes
Outstanding rating	Unrated

Market comment

AEPCO picked a stable market and kept co-manager commitments down to 2 million. Nevertheless, demand was already beginning to thin. The deal was considered fairly priced at 63 basis points over the curve, and tightened in a couple of basis points before the government rally. Japanese demand underpinned the issue but some houses still did not find placement a foregone conclusion.

Year	Swap spread semi-annual	Government bond yield semi-annual
1	47/42	9.000
2	52/47	9.080
3	62/57	9.180
4	63/58	9.250
5	65/60	9.310

The issuer's cash flow resulting from the bond issue is as follows:

	Interest	Principal	Total
	−149,625,000.00		−149,625,000.00
Year 1	14,625,000.00		14,625,000.00
Year 2	14,625,000.00		14,625,000.00
Year 3	14,625,000.00	50,000,000.00	64,625,000.00
Year 4	9,750,000.00	50,000,000.00	59,750,000.00
Year 5	4,875,000.00	50,000,000.00	54,875,000.00

The borrower's cost of funds is 9.829% per annum 30/360. Interest on the borrower's cash flow is 9.75% of 150,000,000 for the first three years, then 9.75% of 100,000,000 in the fourth year and 9.75% of 50,000,000 in the final year.

	f	CLx	
149,625,000.00		CHS	STO 0
14,625,000.00		STO 1	
14,625,000.00		STO 2	
64,625,000.00		STO 3	
59,750,000.00		STO 4	
54,875,000.00		STO 5	
5		n	
f		FV/IRR	

Assuming that the issuer is paid the bid side of the swap market, then the swap rates in the one to five years, and their zero coupon equivalents would be as follows:

Governments	Spread	Semi-annual	Annual	Zero
9.000	0.420	9.420	9.642	9.642
9.080	0.470	9.550	9.778	9.785
9.180	0.570	9.750	9.988	10.014
9.250	0.580	9.830	10.072	10.106
9.310	0.600	9.910	10.156	10.202

The offered side of the swap rates, and their zero coupon equivalents would be as follows:

Governments	Spread	Semi-annual	Annual	Zero
9.000	0.470	9.470	9.694	9.694
9.080	0.520	9.600	9.830	9.837
9.180	0.620	9.800	10.040	10.066
9.250	0.630	9.880	10.124	10.158
9.310	0.650	9.960	10.208	10.254

In order to hedge the amortizing structure, the swap counterparty will need to enter into three swaps on a notional principal amount of 50,000,000 in each case. The first swap will have a maturity of three years, the second a maturity of four years and the third a maturity of five years. There will therefore be 150,000,000 outstanding in the first three years, 100,000,000 in the fourth year when the 3-year swap matures, and 50,000,000 in the final year when the 4-year swap matures.

To calculate the breakeven rate required in the amortizing structure calculate the interest payments due to the swap market maker in the three hedging swaps. The swap counterparty receives the bid side of the market, the lower rates, as the transactions are executed at her request. So the cash flows are as follows:

9.988	50,000,000.00	4,994,000.00
10.072	50,000,000.00	5,036,000.00
10.156	50,000,000.00	5,078,000.00
Years 1–3	15,108,000.00	
Year 4	10,114,000.00	
Year 5	5,078,000.00	

To calculate the internal rate of return of the amortizing structure, insert the principal amounts:

−150,000,000.00
15,108,000.00
15,108,000.00
65,108,000.00
60,114,000.00
55,078,000.00

The internal rate of return of this cash flow is 10.08357564. So the breakeven amortizing swap rate is about 10.084% per annum 30/360. If the swap counterparty paid this rate in return for Libor flat, then the net cash flows resulting from the hedge would be as follows:

	Swap	Hedge	Net
10.084*150,000,000=	−15,126,000.00	15,108,000.00	−18,000.00
10.084*150,000,000=	−15,126,000.00	15,108,000.00	−18,000.00
10.084*150,000,000=	−15,126,000.00	15,108,000.00	−18,000.00
10.084*100,000,000=	−10,084,000.00	10,114,000.00	30,000.00
10.084* 50,000,000=	−5,042,000.00	5,078,000.00	36,000.00

The principle employed in hedging an amortizing swap transaction is to balance the net present value of the hedge against the net present value of the flows required by the customer. The trader needs to ask "how much am I being asked to pay out?" and "what is the value of the flows I receive in the hedge?" In this case the answer lies in the latter question. Having established what revenues are available from the three hedging swaps, it is then possible to calculate what the breakeven rate payable to the customer is.

In principle all swap structures are arranged by answering these questions. In a plain vanilla, or generic swap, the net value of the transaction is approximately zero, the precise value is the bid/offer spread. In an amortizing swap, or any other structure, the same is true. The attractive part of the proposition from a market maker's perspective is that the bid/offer spread in an amortizing swap is likely to be wider than in a generic swap, and the values of the cash flows are slightly less transparent.

Hedging floating rates

In contrast to hedging a fixed-rate cash flow, the management of floating-rate flows deals with the notional principal amount rather than the discounted value of the coupon payments.

A trader has entered into the following transactions:

Pay fixed 2-year US$ 25 million
Receive fixed 7-year US$ 10 million

The trader's net floating-rate position is therefore US$ 15 million. This is the amount which needs to be hedged.

The most frequently used hedge for the floating side of US dollar interest rate swaps is the 3-month eurodollar futures contract. When hedging a 6-month floating rate, it is necessary to double the number of contracts bought or sold or alternatively, to divide them between the first two settlement dates, i.e., if a trader wants to hedge a US$ 15 million position, he could sell 30 contracts for June or 15 for June and 15 for September. This does not represent a perfect hedge, but then it is not possible to enter into futures contracts for fractions of US$ 1 million. The 3-month eurodollar futures contract is based on US$ 1,000,000 for 90 days over a base of 360 days. So the tick value of the contract is US$ 25 million. This is the profit or loss on one contract if interest rates move by 0.01%:

$$US\$\ 1,000,000 * 90/360 * 0.01\%$$

Interest rate swaps and forward rate agreements

There are three interest rate components to a 1-year interest rate swap from an annual fixed rate to 6-month Libor:

- The annual fixed rate
- The first Libor payment (months 1–6)
- The second Libor payment (months 7–12)

Assume a trader receives a fixed rate and pays the floating rates. We can establish the income (fixed) and the first part of the expenditure (floating) at the time the deal is struck as both the fixed rate and the first Libor rate are known.

For example, we agree to pay 6-month Libor for a period of one year against a receipt of 8.5% p.a. on a money market basis. The notional principal amount of the transaction is 10 million. 6-month Libor for the first period is 7.75% s.a. (money market basis) and there are 182 days in the period.

If we calculate the income for the year and the expenditure for the first six months, we will know the trader's break-even expenditure for the second floating payment:

$$10,000,000.00*8.5/100*365/360$$
$$= 861,805.56\ (cash\ +)$$

$$10,000,000.00*7.75/100*182/360$$
$$= 391,805.56\ (cash\ -)$$

There is therefore a surplus of 470,000.00 available to cover interest for the second Libor period covering months 7 to 12.

In order to calculate the true break-even, however, it is necessary to allow for the cost of funding the first Libor payment for the remainder of the year. A payment of 391,805.56 is made after six months but the receipt of 861,805.56 does not occur until the end of the 12th month. It is therefore necessary to pay interest on 391,805.56 at the Libor rate for the second 6-month period.

The break-even rate can therefore be calculated as follows:

$$470,000.00 = (p*i*183/360) + (i*183/360*391,805.56)$$

where:

$$p = \text{principal amount } (10,000,000.00)$$
i = interest for the second Libor period (months 7–12) expressed as a decimal.

The first set of brackets represents the interest due in the second period. The second set of brackets is the interest due in the second period on the amount of interest paid in the first Libor period. It is important to understand that a floating-rate payment is made at the end of six months and no fixed interest is received until the end of the year. The second set of brackets represents the funding cost.

Multiplying both sides of the equation by 360/183 produces the following:

$$470,000.00*360/183$$
$$=(P*i) + (i*391,805.56)$$

Removing i from the brackets:

$$= i \, (P + 391,805.56)$$

or

$$= i \, (10,391,805.56)$$

Dividing both sides of the equation by 10,391,805.56 determines the maximum interest rate payable for the second Libor period:

$$\text{US\$ } 470,000.00*360/183$$
$$= 924,590.16/10,391,805.56$$
$$= 0.088973$$

So the break-even is 8.8973%. The maximum rate for the second Libor period would therefore be 8⅞%. If an FRA was more expensive than this, the transaction would be unprofitable.

The general formula for calculating the breakeven Libor in the second period is therefore:

$$\frac{(\text{FXD}i - \text{1st } i) \times 360/\text{days}}{1 + \text{1st } i}$$

where:

1st i = Interest rate in first Libor period, expressed as a decimal and adjusted for the number of days, e.g., *182/360

FXD i = Fixed rate expressed as a decimal, adjusted for days

Days = Number of days in second Libor period

So using the numbers from the example above gives the following:

$$\frac{(0.086187 - 0.03918) \times 360/183}{1 + 0.03918}$$
$$= 0.088973$$

So our break-even is 8.8973%. Our maximum rate for the second Libor period would therefore be 8⅞%. If an FRA was more expensive than this, the transaction would be unprofitable.

It is often the case, however, that Libor rollover dates do not match. We might, for example enter into a 1-year swap today (against 6-month Libor) and a reverse or matching transaction tomorrow. If the Libor rollovers were mismatched by one day we would need to buy or sell futures today, six months from today and one year from today. These hedges could be reversed on the following day protecting us from adverse moves in Libor, assuming a perfect correlation between cash and futures.

Relationship with forward rate agreements (FRAs)

Interest rate swaps are sometimes described as being equivalent to a series of FRAs: FRAs are sometimes described as single period interest rate swaps.

An FRA, or forward rate agreement, is an over-the-counter derivative contract which allows a buyer to fix the cost of debt from one forward date to another.

> **Buying an FRA is equivalent to paying fixed in a swap.**

The return from an investment can be fixed by selling an FRA.

> **Selling an FRA is equivalent to receiving fixed in a swap.**

The price of FRAs is influenced by the slope of the yield curve and therefore reflects what futures traders and commodity dealers refer to as "the cost of carry." Let's suppose that you want to buy gold in one year's time at a price to be set today. The seller of the gold can either agree a price with you today and leave an open position, or bet that he is going to make a profit. Alternatively as a market maker he could cover his position by buying the gold today at the prevailing spot price and keep it for one year until the date when you have agreed to take delivery. A decision to do this incurs the cost of storage, insurance and financing, as the market maker needs to pay for the gold now and will not receive any money from you until the delivery date. These costs are the cost of carry, and in an efficient market the forward price is the sum of the spot price and the cost of carry. The foreign exchange markets in the major currencies are good examples of efficient markets and in the forward dollar/euro market, for example, the forward prices out to one year usually equate precisely to the cost of carry.

Compare the financial effects of a series of FRAs with a 1-year interest rate swap looking at the similarities and the differences. A treasurer has funded the company on a floating-rate basis at 3-month Libor and bought a series of FRAs to change the company's exposure to interest rate risk from a floating- to a fixed-rate basis at the following prices:

3-month Libor	6.250%	91 days
3 v 6 FRA	6.375%	92 days
6 v 9 FRA	6.500%	91 days
9 v 12 FRA	6.750%	91 days

The annualized cost of funds is calculated by multiplying together the factors produced by expressing each rate as a decimal, multiplying it by the number of days in the 3-month funding period, dividing by the basis of 360 and adding 1:

$$(1+0.0625*91/360)(1+0.06375*92/360)(1+0.065*91/360)$$
$$(1+0.0675*91/360)$$
$$= 1.0158*1.0163*1.0164*1.0171$$
$$= 1.06723$$
$$= 6.723\%$$

The first factor tells us how much principal and interest will be outstanding after the first three months. So if the company borrows US$ 100 million it will owe US$ 101,580,000 after three months. This amount could be used as the hedge amount: the company could buy this amount of FRAs.

Multiplying the first two factors together tells us how much principal and interest will be outstanding at the end of six months: US$ 103,235,754 (1.0158*1.0163). As above, this can be used as the hedge amount.

Multiplying the first three factors together tells us how much principal and interest will be outstanding at the end of nine months: US$ 104,928,820. This can also be used as the hedge amount.

Multiplying all the factors tells us the total principal and interest outstanding at the end of the year: 106,723,103 and therefore that the swap rates which break-even to an FRA hedge are 6.723% on a bond equivalent basis (30/360) or 6.631% on a money market basis (actual/360), (6.723*360/365).

EXAMPLE ## FRAs and interest rate swaps

Eurocurrency rates

3 months	8.25/8.375	91 days
3v6	8.50/8.625	91 days
6v9	8.875/9.00	91 days
9v12	8.875/9.00	92 days

1-year swap: 8.875/9.00 (against 3-month Libor)

All rates are quoted on a money market basis.

If a treasurer wants to change floating-rate funds to a fixed rate basis, which is cheaper, the 1-year swap (paying a fixed rate) or a 3-month funding position with the purchase of FRAs for the appropriate periods? What amount of FRAs would the treasurer need to purchase in the 9v12 in order to be fully hedged?

The cost of fixed-rate funds for one year through the swap is 9.125% per annum 30/360 (9 * 365/360)

Using the FRAs would be more expensive:

$$1.021170*1.021802*1.02275*1.023$$
$$= 1.0917168$$
$$= 9.17168\% \text{ p.a. } 30/360$$

There is a very close relationship between the pricing of swaps and the pricing of FRAs and futures. It is from this relationship that the value of floating-rate cash flows can be most effectively viewed. Another perspective on the value of floating-rate cash flows can be seen by looking at the market methodology for valuing FRNs, or floating-rate notes.

Valuing floating-rate notes

Pricing floating-rate notes is, in principal, like pricing fixed-rate debt: establish the cash flows, discount them to their present values to determine the **dirty price**, then subtract accrued interest to calculate the **clean price**.

There are however a number of differences in the detail. The yield to maturity on a floater, or the discount rate, is called the **discount margin**. There are usually at least two discount rates used in the pricing of floaters. First the coupons are discounted to the next coupon payment date at the discount margin, then the next coupon is added and the total is discounted at the money market rate from settlement to the next coupon payment date.

The market practice is to use the current Libor as a benchmark for the discount margin. So if, for example, a floater has a discount margin of 6-month Libor + 25 basis points and the current 6-month Libor is 5.50, then the discount rate would be 5.75%.

Maturity	1 year 47 days
Coupon	6-month Libor + 30
6-month Libor	5.75
47-day rate	5.55
Next coupon	6.30
Current coupon period	183 days
Discount margin	6-month Libor + 50

The first coupon is 6.30% semi-annually for 183 days or 3.2025%:

$$6.30\% * 183/360 = 3.2025$$

The next two coupons are 6.05% semi-annually (5.75% + 0.30%) for 182.5 days. Some people use the actual number of days, but 182.5 is a commonly used approximation.

$$6.05\% * 182.5/360 = 3.067\%$$

The cash flows are now established:

1st coupon	3.2025
2nd coupon	3.0670
P + last coupon	103.0670

Next the second and third cash flows are discounted to the next coupon payment date at the discount margin of Libor + 50 or 6.25% (5.75% + 0.50%):

$$3.067/[1 + (0.0625 * 182.5/360)] = 2.973$$

		Value at next coupon
1st coupon	3.2025	3.2025
2nd coupon	3.0670	2.9730
P + last coupon	103.0670	96.8340

$$103.067/(1 + (0.0625 * 182.5/360))^2 = 96.834\%$$

		Value at next coupon
1st coupon	3.2025	3.2025
2nd coupon	3.0670	2.9730
P + last coupon	103.0670	96.8340
		103.0095

So the value of the floater at the next coupon payment date is 103.01%.

n	i	PV	PMT	FV
2	3.168	−99.8100	3.07	100.00
		−3.2025		
		−103.0125		

Discounting this at the 47-day rate gives a dirty price of 102.27%:

$$103.01\%/[1 + (0.0555 * 47/360)] = 102.27\%$$

Accrued interest is 2.38%:

$$6.30\% * 136/360 = 2.38\%$$

So the **clean price** is 99.89%.

What is the clean price of this floating-rate note?

Maturity	2 years 98 days
Coupon	6-month Libor + 25
6-month Libor	6.00
98-day rate	5.90
Next coupon	6.15
Current coupon period	183 days
Discount margin	6-month Libor + 10

Using an assumed index of 6.00%, the current 6-month Libor, then future coupons will be 6.25%, which, assuming 182.5 days in each coupon period produces cash flows of 3.17%:

$$6.125 * 182.5/360$$
$$= 3.17\%$$

Discount the principal amount and the four full coupons back to the next coupon payment date at the discount margin, Libor + 10:

$$\text{Discount rate} = 6.10 * 182.5/360$$
$$= 3.09\%$$

n	i	PV	PMT	FV
4	3.09	−100.30	3.17	100.00

So the value of the full coupons at the next coupon payment date is 100.30%. Add the first coupon, 3.13% (6.15% * 183/360) to give the value of the floater at the next coupon payment date:

$$100.30\% + 3.13\% = 103.43\%$$

Discount the value of the floater at the next coupon at the financing rate from settlement to the next coupon, 5.9% for 98 days:

$$103.43\%/1 + (0.059 * 98/360)$$
$$= 101.80\%$$

This is the dirty, or full, price of the FRN. Interest accrues for 85 days from the last coupon to the settlement date (183 − 98). Subtract accrued interest of 1.45% (6.15 * 85/360) to calculate the clean price of the FRN:

$$= 101.80\% - 1.45\%$$
$$= 100.35\%$$

Exercise | **Pricing a floating-rate note (2-year)**

Calculate the price of this floating-rate note:

- Current coupon (4¾%)
- Number of days in current coupon period (182 days)
- Days remaining from settlement date to next coupon payment date (57 days)
- Spread in relation to Libor (plus ½%)
- Assumed base Libor for the life (5%)
- Financing rate from settlement date to next coupon payment date (5.3%)
- Years remaining to maturity (assume this was a 2-year FRN, 125 days ago)
- Number of compounding periods between now and maturity (4 periods)
- Coupon reset frequency (every 6 months)
- Coupon payment frequency (every 6 months)
- Discount margin (Libor plus 70 basis points)

Answer | Determine the outstanding cash flows using the assumed base Libor rate plus the spread (5% + ½%):

$$(0.0475*182/360)+(0.055*182.5/360)+(0.055*182.5/360)+$$
$$(1+(0.055*182.5/360))$$

Discount the last three cash flows to the next coupon date, using the discount margin (expressed as an annual bond equivalent rate) as a discount rate:

$$(0.055*182.5/360)/(1+0.05862)\char`^0.5 = 0.0271$$
$$(0.055*182.5/360)/(1+0.05862)\char`^1 = 0.02634$$
$$((1+(0.055*182.5/360)))/(1+0.05862)\char`^1.5 = 0.94369$$

This gives a total of 0.99713.

Add the first cash flow $(0.0475*182.5/360 = 0.02401)$ to this total. This reflects the future value of the future cash flows on the next coupon payment date:

$$0.99713 + 0.02401 = 1.02114 \text{ or } 102.114\%$$

Discount the future value of the future cash flows to their present value using the financing rate from settlement to next coupon as the discount rate:

$$1.02114/(1+(0.053*57/360)) = 1.01264$$

This tells us the full or the dirty price for the FRN. To calculate the clean price we need to subtract accrued interest:

$$0.0475*125/360 = 0.0165$$

So the clean price of the FRN is 99.614% (1.01264 – 0.0165)

First coupon	4.75	Days in 1st coupon	182
Spread	0.5	Days to next coupon	57
Assumed index	5	Accrued interest	1.649
Financing rate	5.3		
DM	0.7		

	1st	2nd	3rd	4th
FRN Cash flows	2.401	2.788	2.788	102.788
Value of cash flows at next coupon	2.401	2.710	2.634	94.369
Value of FRN at next coupon	102.114			

Dirty price	101.264
Clean price	99.615

The value of the FRN at the next coupon is the sum of the first coupon payment and the discounted values of the subsequent coupons and payment of principal. The dirty price is the present value of the value of the FRN at the next coupon discounted at the financing rate. The clean price is, as usual, the dirty price less accrued interest.

In the example above the cash flows were discounted using the annual 30/360 rate. For a 6-monthly discount, the square root of this number was taken. The same answer can be derived by using the semi-annual money market (act/360) rate and squaring it for the i year discount and raising it to the power of three for the 18-month discount.

Exercise

Calculate the discount rate by multiplying the discount margin by 182.5/360:

$$(0.057*182.5/360)/(1+(0.057*182.5/360)) = 0.0271$$
$$(0.057*182.5/360)/(1+(0.057*182.5/360))^2 = 0.02634$$
$$(1+(0.057*182/360))/(1+(0.057*182.5/360))^3 = 0.94369$$

Answer

This gives a total of 0.99713, as in the example above. It really is a question of whether a cash flow manager prefers to use the semi-annual rates compounded, or the annual rates discounted.

In both of the examples above the floater was valued using a single discount rate. This is consistent with rule 803.1 for valuing fixed-rate bonds. This time a single interest rate at the short end of the curve, 6-month Libor plus the discount margin, is used as the discount rate rather than a maturity rate as in the case of a fixed-rate bond. So in each case there are the assumptions that the yield curve is flat and it will not move. While this is a good indicator of the value of a floater when a floater is trading close to par, it is not such a good indicator of the price when a floater moves significantly away from par. Under these circumstances, it would be more appropriate to value the floater using a series of forward rates to discount each cash flow back to the previous coupon period. These forward rates could be a strip of FRA prices which is equivalent to a swap of the same maturity. So a better estimate of the value of a floater can be calculated by using the swap rate of the same maturity as the floater as the assumed index, instead of 3- or 6-month Libor.

Hedging swap transactions

Maturity	Spread	Governments
2	70/75	9.2
3	80/85	9.4
4	80/85	9.4
5	80/85	9.7
7	75/80	9.75
10	75/80	9.8

A customer calls you, in your capacity as an interest rate swap market maker, and asks for 2–10-year prices. You quote the above prices. Your customer wants to pay you a fixed rate (p.a. 30/360) of interest in each maturity on a notional principal amount of 25 million. As you have the necessary limits available, you agree to be a receiver in the six transactions.

Question

If you decide to hedge your fixed-rate positions, short term, using one 5-year swap, how much do you need to transact?

After transacting the 5-year swap, what is your floating-rate position?

Maturity	Rate	PV (%)	PV (cash)
2	10.20	17.66	10,980,000.00
3	10.51	25.90	16,110,000.00
4	10.51	32.95	20,491,000.00
5	10.83	40.20	25,000,000.00
7	10.83	51.32	31,920,000.00
10	10.88	64.40	40,050,000.00
			144,551,000.00

In order to hedge 25,000,000 2 year it is necessary to swap about 11,000,000 5 year. In order to hedge the total 150,000,000 (6* 25,000,000) it is necessary to deal in 145,000,000 5 year.

The net floating-rate position would then be 5,000,000: 150 million – 145 million. The market maker would be a payer of 150 million on a floating-rate basis, being a receiver of fixed, and a receiver of 145 million on a floating-rate basis in the hedge transaction. The risk to the market maker is that Libor will fall between now and when a reversing or matching floating-rate transaction is put in place. This could, for example, happen on the following working day. So at the end of each trading day, the net floating-rate exposure needs to be hedged until at least the following day. It is important to understand that it is not necessary to hedge floating exposures in the forward periods. A paradox of floating rates is that there is no exposure to them until the rate is set and the floating rate effectively becomes a fixed rate.

The trader could hedge this exposure to Libor falling between today and tomorrow by either buying futures contracts or selling FRAs. The liquidity in futures is likely to mean a narrower bid/offer spread, and this is likely to be much more important to the trader than the basis risk in the futures hedge. The futures dates are unlikely to coincide exactly with the floating-rate periods so the trader would not have a perfect hedge. But since the swap book is not perfectly hedged anyway this is unlikely to be a deciding factor in choosing the short term hedge instrument. As the trader is likely to be moving in and out of the floating-rate hedge each day, sometimes reversing positions taken the previous day, liquidity is likely to be more important than precision. For traders, or hedgers, for whom precision is more important, then FRAs are an ideal hedging tool.

Hedging a structured product

Borrowers are sometimes offered structures by their investment banks, often because there is strong demand by investors for a particular view. When interest rates are expected to fall it is sometimes possible to persuade floating-rate investors to buy a reverse floating-rate note. As the name suggests, instead of benefiting as interest rates rise, which is the case with conventional floating-rate notes, purchasers of reverse FRNs benefit as rates fall. This is achieved by offering a coupon consisting of a fixed rate less a floating rate. In this case, for example, the coupon is 16.75% minus 6-month Libor. So as Libor rises the coupon paid to investors falls. Another temptation often offered as an incentive to investors to buy reverse floaters is a higher than market fixed-rate coupon at the start of the deal. Here investors are offered 12.5% semi-annually for the first two years and 16.75% minus 6-month Libor for the remaining five years of the transaction.

Borrower's motivation

Almost every structured note which is issued is swapped so that the borrower does not have the opposite risk from the investors. In this case this means that the borrower does not, net, pay a fixed rate for two years and then 16.75% minus 6-month Libor for the remaining life of the deal. While the borrower pays these gross flows to investors, the swap counterparty hedges these flows leaving the borrower with a transaction often at very attractive sub-Libor levels. So the borrower is arbitraging the price of the structure as a unit, sold to investors, and its value in its component parts in the swap market.

Hedgers' thought processes

The general approach to hedging a structure is to try to reduce the swap book to the smallest residual risk. So at each stage of the process the swap market maker will attempt to reduce the overall exposure. This is the same as the approach used in pricing an amortizing swap. The idea is to leave the book with as little variable risk as possible while capturing the bid/offer spread.

Amount	500 million
Maturity	7 years
Issue price	101.50%
Fixed price re-offer	100.00%
Coupons years 1 & 2	12.5% semi annually
Coupons years 3 – 7	16.75% – 6-month Libor
Cap	0.35%
2 year swap	10.20/10.30 s.a. act/365
7 year swap	9.80/9.90 s.a. act/365

The swap counterparty hedging this issue wants to offer the borrower an all-in cost of floating-rate funds of 6-month Libor minus 40 basis points and to determine what would be the remaining revenue for the swap book once this transaction is hedged.

The hedger first calculates the payments required by the borrower to match the bond issue:

Year	Coupons	Coupons	Floating receipt
0.5	−12.5/2		+(6m Libor − 40)
1	−12.5/2		+(6m Libor − 40)
1.5	−12.5/2		+(6m Libor − 40)
2	−12.5/2		+(6m Libor − 40)
2.5	−16.75/2	+6m Libor	+(6m Libor − 40)
3	−16.75/2	+6m Libor	+(6m Libor − 40)
3.5	−16.75/2	+6m Libor	+(6m Libor − 40)
4	−16.75/2	+6m Libor	+(6m Libor − 40)
4.5	−16.75/2	+6m Libor	+(6m Libor − 40)
5	−16.75/2	+6m Libor	+(6m Libor − 40)
5.5	−16.75/2	+6m Libor	+(6m Libor − 40)
6	−16.75/2	+6m Libor	+(6m Libor − 40)
6.5	−16.75/2	+6m Libor	+(6m Libor − 40)
7	−16.75/2	+6m Libor	+(6m Libor − 40)

In order to hedge the bond issue the borrower needs to be paid 12.50% semi-annually in the first four coupon periods. Thereafter the borrower is effectively paid 16.75% semi-annually and the swap counterparty effectively is paid 6-month Libor. While this is not the reality, it is a convenient way of expressing 16.75% minus 6-month Libor. It makes the structure of the cash flows clearer to the hedger. In return for these flows the borrower will pay the swap counterparty 6-month Libor minus 40 basis points.

The swap counterparty needs to receive a fixed rate in a 7-year swap in order to cover the floating-rate payments from the borrower. If the trader deals at 9.80 semi-annually, then the swap book's position will be as follows:

Year	Coupons	Coupons	Floating receipt	7 yr fxd	7 yr ftg
0.5	−12.5/2		+(6m Libor − 40)	+9.8/2	−6m Libor
1	−12.5/2		+(6m Libor − 40)	+9.8/2	−6m Libor
1.5	−12.5/2		+(6m Libor − 40)	+9.8/2	−6m Libor
2	−12.5/2		+(6m Libor − 40)	+9.8/2	−6m Libor
2.5	−16.75/2	+6m Libor	+(6m Libor − 40)	+9.8/2	−6m Libor
3	−16.75/2	+6m Libor	+(6m Libor − 40)	+9.8/2	−6m Libor
3.5	−16.75/2	+6m Libor	+(6m Libor − 40)	+9.8/2	−6m Libor
4	−16.75/2	+6m Libor	+(6m Libor − 40)	+9.8/2	−6m Libor
4.5	−16.75/2	+6m Libor	+(6m Libor − 40)	+9.8/2	−6m Libor
5	−16.75/2	+6m Libor	+(6m Libor − 40)	+9.8/2	−6m Libor
5.5	−16.75/2	+6m Libor	+(6m Libor − 40)	+9.8/2	−6m Libor
6	−16.75/2	+6m Libor	+(6m Libor − 40)	+9.8/2	−6m Libor
6.5	−16.75/2	+6m Libor	+(6m Libor − 40)	+9.8/2	−6m Libor
7	−16.75/2	+6m Libor	+(6m Libor − 40)	+9.8/2	−6m Libor

Netting the cash flows produces the following.

Year	Coupons	Ftg receipt	Net fxd
0.5		−0.2	−1.35
1		−0.2	−1.35
1.5		−0.2	−1.35
2		−0.2	−1.35
2.5	+6m Libor	−0.2	−3.475
3	+6m Libor	−0.2	−3.475
3.5	+6m Libor	−0.2	−3.475
4	+6m Libor	−0.2	−3.475
4.5	+6m Libor	−0.2	−3.475
5	+6m Libor	−0.2	−3.475
5.5	+6m Libor	−0.2	−3.475
6	+6m Libor	−0.2	−3.475
6.5	+6m Libor	−0.2	−3.475
7	+6m Libor	−0.2	−3.475

Note that 6-month Libor minus 40, actual 365, is equivalent to 20 basis points in each semi-annual period. In the first two years the swap market maker receives 9.80% semi-annually and pays 12.5% semi-annually. This nets to a payment of 1.35%:

$$+9.8\%/2 - 12.5\%/2$$
$$= +4.9\% - 6.25\%$$
$$= -1.35\%$$

In the remaining five years, the swap market maker pays 16.75% semi-annually and continues to receive 9.8% semi-annually. This nets to a payment of 3.475%:

$$+ 9.8\%/2 - 16.75\%/2$$
$$= +4.9\% - 8.375\%$$
$$= 3.475\%$$

The swap counterparty now has a forward/forward floating-rate exposure left to hedge. This exposure starts in two years and runs for five years. It is possible to cover this floating-rate position by paying a floating rate for seven years and receiving a floating rate for two years:

Year	Coupons	7 yr	2 yr
0.5		−6m Libor	+6m Libor
1		−6m Libor	+6m Libor
1.5		−6m Libor	+6m Libor
2		−6m Libor	+6m Libor
2.5	+6m Libor	−6m Libor	
3	+6m Libor	−6m Libor	
3.5	+6m Libor	−6m Libor	
4	+6m Libor	−6m Libor	
4.5	+6m Libor	−6m Libor	
5	+6m Libor	−6m Libor	
5.5	+6m Libor	−6m Libor	
6	+6m Libor	−6m Libor	
6.5	+6m Libor	−6m Libor	
7	+6m Libor	−6m Libor	

Entering into a 7-year swap as a payer of floating, a receiver of fixed at 9.8% semi-annually, and a 2-year swap receiving floating and paying a fixed rate of 10.3% semi-annually, eliminates the swap book runner's floating cash flows and leaves the following fixed-rate flows:

Year	Ftg receipt	Net fxd	2 yr	7 yr
0.5	−0.2	−1.35	−10.3/2	+9.8/2
1	−0.2	−1.35	−10.3/2	+9.8/2
1.5	−0.2	−1.35	−10.3/2	+9.8/2
2	−0.2	−1.35	−10.3/2	+9.8/2
2.5	−0.2	−3.475		+9.8/2
3	−0.2	−3.475		+9.8/2
3.5	−0.2	−3.475		+9.8/2
4	−0.2	−3.475		+9.8/2
4.5	−0.2	−3.475		+9.8/2
5	−0.2	−3.475		+9.8/2
5.5	−0.2	−3.475		+9.8/2
6	−0.2	−3.475		+9.8/2
6.5	−0.2	−3.475		+9.8/2
7	−0.2	−3.475		+9.8/2

The floating receipt and the net fixed columns are as before and the market maker now has the fixed-rate cash flows from the 2- and 7-year swaps. Netting the fixed-rate cash flows above leaves the swap trader with the following:

Year	Ftg receipt	Net fxd
0.5	−0.2	−1.6
1	−0.2	−1.6
1.5	−0.2	−1.6
2	−0.2	−1.6
2.5	−0.2	1.425
3	−0.2	1.425
3.5	−0.2	1.425
4	−0.2	1.425
4.5	−0.2	1.425
5	−0.2	1.425
5.5	−0.2	1.425
6	−0.2	1.425
6.5	−0.2	1.425
7	−0.2	1.425

Netting the fixed- and the residual floating-rate cash flow leaves the swap book runner with the following cash flow:

Year	Net/Net	Year	Net/Net
0.5	−1.8	4	1.225
1	−1.8	4.5	1.225
1.5	−1.8	5	1.225
2	−1.8	5.5	1.225
2.5	1.225	6	1.225
3	1.225	6.5	1.225
3.5	1.225	7	1.225

There is another consideration in hedging this position. The borrower will pay 16.75% – 6-month Libor to the investors. If Libor rises above 16.75%, then the borrower will pay a coupon of 0% to the investors. So it is accurate to say that the swap counterparty pays 16.75% in return for 6-month Libor as long as Libor is below 16.75%. If Libor rises above this level, the swap book runner will have a mismatch because the Libor "receipt" from the borrower has a ceiling of 16.75%. It is therefore necessary for the market maker to buy a Libor cap at 16.75% in order to hedge this risk. If the cap costs 0.35% flat, then the swap book runner's net cash flow becomes as follows:

Year	Net/Net	Year	Net/Net
0	−0.35	4	1.225
0.5	−1.8	4.5	1.225
1	−1.8	5	1.225
1.5	−1.8	5.5	1.225
2	−1.8	6	1.225
2.5	1.225	6.5	1.225
3	1.225	7	1.225
3.5	1.225		

This net cash flow is the result of the transactions in the chart below. The first three columns are the payments to and from the borrower, the next four columns represent the fixed and floating payments from two 7-year swaps and the last two columns represent the fixed and floating cash flows from the 2-year swap. So the hedge for this transaction involves the following:

- two 7-year swaps
- one 2-year swap
- one cap purchase

Year	Coupons	Coupons	Floating receipt	7 yr fxd	7 yr ftg	7 yr fxd	7 yr ftg	2 yr fxd	2 yr ftg
0.5	−12.5/2		+(6m Libor − 40)	+9.8/2	−6m Libor	+9.8/2	−6m Libor	−10.3/2	+6m Libor
1	−12.5/2		+(6m Libor − 40)	+9.8/2	−6m Libor	+9.8/2	−6m Libor	−10.3/2	+6m Libor
1.5	−12.5/2		+(6m Libor − 40)	+9.8/2	−6m Libor	+9.8/2	−6m Libor	−10.3/2	+6m Libor
2	−12.5/2		+(6m Libor − 40)	+9.8/2	−6m Libor	+9.8/2	−6m Libor	−10.3/2	+6m Libor
2.5	−16.75/2	+6m Libor	+(6m Libor − 40)	+9.8/2	−6m Libor	+9.8/2	−6m Libor		
3	−16.75/2	+6m Libor	+(6m Libor − 40)	+9.8/2	−6m Libor	+9.8/2	−6m Libor		
3.5	−16.75/2	+6m Libor	+(6m Libor − 40)	+9.8/2	−6m Libor	+9.8/2	−6m Libor		
4	−16.75/2	+6m Libor	+(6m Libor − 40)	+9.8/2	−6m Libor	+9.8/2	−6m Libor		
4.5	−16.75/2	+6m Libor	+(6m Libor − 40)	+9.8/2	−6m Libor	+9.8/2	−6m Libor		
5	−16.75/2	+6m Libor	+(6m Libor − 40)	+9.8/2	−6m Libor	+9.8/2	−6m Libor		
5.5	−16.75/2	+6m Libor	+(6m Libor − 40)	+9.8/2	−6m Libor	+9.8/2	−6m Libor		
6	−16.75/2	+6m Libor	+(6m Libor − 40)	+9.8/2	−6m Libor	+9.8/2	−6m Libor		
6.5	−16.75/2	+6m Libor	+(6m Libor − 40)	+9.8/2	−6m Libor	+9.8/2	−6m Libor		
7	−16.75/2	+6m Libor	+(6m Libor − 40)	+9.8/2	−6m Libor	+9.8/2	−6m Libor		

	f	CLx	
0.35	CHS	STO	0
1.8	CHS	STO	1
1.8	CHS	STO	2
1.8	CHS	STO	3
1.8	CHS	STO	4
1.225		STO	5
1.225		STO	6
1.225		STO	7
1.225		STO	8
1.225		STO	9
1.225		STO	10
1.225		STO	11
1.225		STO	12
1.225		STO	13
1.225		STO	14
	14	n	
	f	IRR	

The cash flow has an internal rate of return of 7.289%. This is the flat rate for the semi-annual periods so the semi-annual equivalent rate is 14.578% (2 * 7.289%). As this is much higher than the market rates the swap market maker has a positive net present value of the cash flow. Discounting the cash flow at the offered side of the 7-year swap rate gives a net present value of 1.076%:

	f	CLx	
0.35	CHS	STO	0
1.8	CHS	STO	1
1.8	CHS	STO	2
1.8	CHS	STO	3
1.8	CHS	STO	4
1.225		STO	5
1.225		STO	6
1.225		STO	7
1.225		STO	8
1.225		STO	9
1.225		STO	10
1.225		STO	11
1.225		STO	12
1.225		STO	13
1.225		STO	14
	14	n	
	4.95	i	
	f	NPV	

This value of 1.076% is the market maker's surplus after hedging the cash flows outlined above. Against the 1.076%, or in cash terms 5,380,000, the market maker needs to provide for credit risk in the payments to the issuer and the swap and cap hedges, and the cost of the capital employed in the transaction.

It is sometimes said that structured products are not an efficient way to take the particular exposure which is offered in them. In this case investors are offered the same directional exposure as a fixed-rate bond, but they are offered it in a much more complex way and at a much wider bid/offer spread than is likely to prevail for a fixed-rate bond issued by the same credit. So why would an investor take such a risk? Given the choice of a reverse floater or a fixed-rate bond, surely a rational investor would always pick the fixed-rate bond? While this is true in theory the markets do not always operate in an efficient way. Not all investors are allowed to buy fixed-rate bonds. A money market fund may be permitted to buy reverse floaters but not fixed-rate debt. So it is not a question of the most efficient way of taking this view on rates. It may simply be that this is the only way an investor can express this view.

Unwinding existing swaps

To unwind a swap, assume you enter into a reverse swap (if you are a payer in the original swap, you will be a receiver in the reverse swap) at the prevailing rate for the remaining period of the original swap. Discount the difference between the two swap rates at the reverse rate, and this will determine the necessary payment or receipt required to unwind the original transaction. This process, looking at the net difference between the rate at which the original deal was struck and the current rate for reversing the transaction, is identical to the process used for marking a swap to market.

EXAMPLE Your clients have received fixed rates in the following amounts and maturities. What is the termination value of these transactions?

All swap receipts are against 6-month Libor flat, so for example, NEC receives 14,565,000 p.a. (9.71/100*150,000,000).

Amount	Maturity	Rate p.a. 30/360	C/party
150	2	9.71	NEC
200	6	9.91	AEPCO
200	6	10.01	TMB
150	4	9.93	EDB
150	3	9.85	AEC

Swap rates		
Maturity	Spread (s.a)	Governments (s.a.)
2	55/65	7.32
3	60/70	7.41
4	63/73	7.48
5	65/75	7.55
7	65/75	7.67
10	65/75	7.72

Unwinding swaps: methodology

Nordic Export Credit

First calculate the payment in the original swap. The rate is 9.71% per annum 30/360 on a notional principal amount of 150,000,000. So the payment is 14,565,000:

$$\text{Original swap} = 9.71\% \text{ p.a. } 30/360$$
$$9.71\% * 150,000,000 = 14,565,000$$

So Nordic Export Credit is a receiver of 14,565,00 for the remaining two years of the swap. Next calculate the price at which Nordic Export Credit could reverse this transaction. While it is not usually necessary, or desirable to enter into a reverse swap transaction when terminating or unwinding a swap, it can be useful to think of the termination value in terms of the net difference between the original transaction and a hypothetical reverse transaction executed at current market rates.

The price at which they could pay a fixed rate for two years is 65 over a government yield of 7.32%. Both the swap spread and the government bond yield are expressed as semi-annual rates so the annual equivalent of their sum, 7.97%, is 8.13%. The payment in the reverse swap would be 12,195,000:

$$\text{Reverse swap} = 8.13\% \text{ p.a. } 30/360$$
$$8.13\% * 150,000,000 = 12,195,000$$

The net of these two cash flows is 2,370,000:

$$+14,545,000 - 12,195,000 = +2,370,000 \text{ p.a. for two years}$$

Discounting 2,370,000 at 8.13% produces a present value of 4,218,816.39. This is the payment which would be made to Nordic Export Credit if the swap was terminated, or unwound.

Alternatively, net Nordic Export Credit's original swap rate and the current market rate: $+9.71\% - 8.13\% = 1.58\%$. Discount the 158 basis points per annum to its present value and multiply by the notional principal amount.

n	i	PV	PMT	FV
2	8.13	–2.8125	1.58	0.00

$$PV = 2.8125\% * 150,000,000$$
$$= 4,218,816.39$$

Asian Electric Power Company

The swap rate in the original deal is 9.91% per annum 30/360. The rate in the reverse transaction is 75 over a government yield of 7.61. This is a straight-line interpolation of the 5- and 7-year yields of 7.55 and 7.67. The semi-annual reverse rate is therefore 8.36% and its annual equivalent is 8.53% per annum.

The receipt in the original deal was 19,820,000:

$$200,000,000 * 9.91\%$$

and the payment in the reverse transaction is 17,060,000:

$$+19,820,000 - 17,060,000 = +2,760,000$$

Discounting 2,760,000 per annum for six years at 8.53% gives a present value of **12,556,569.64**

Alternatively, 9.91% – 8.53% = 1.38%. Discount this at the swap rate of 8.53%:

n	i	PV	PMT	FV
6	8.53	–6.278	1.38	0.00

6.278% * 200,000,000 = 12,556,000

The Mortgage Bank

10.01% – 8.53% = 1.48%

n	i	PV	PMT	FV
6	8.53	–6.733	1.48	0.00

6.733% * 200,000,000 = 13,466,465.99

European Development Bank

9.93% – 8.38% = 1.55%

n	i	PV	PMT	FV
4	8.38	–5.091	1.55	0.00

5.091% * 150,000,000 = 7,636,500

Asian Export Credit

9.85% – 8.27% = 1.58%

n	i	PV	PMT	FV
3	8.27	–4.052	1.58	0.00

1.58% * 150,000,000 = 2,370,000

APPENDIX 1
Credit Arbitrage Cases

EXPORT CREDIT BANK

Amount	150,000,000
Maturity	3 years
Coupon	9½% p.a.
Issue price	101⅜%
Amortization	Bullet
Call option	None
Listing	Luxembourg
Denominations	1,000, 10,000
Commissions	1⅝%
Expenses	50,000
Swap	Into floating-rate funds (6-month Libor)
Governing law	English
Negative pledge	Yes
Cross default	Yes
Pari passu	Yes

ECB's third dollar deal of the year was rather aggressive at 46 basis points over the curve but nevertheless offered 4 basis points more than the Asian Export Credit Bank the previous week, generally felt to be a slightly stronger name. The lead manager reported broad institutional placement in Europe as well as in the Middle and Far East.

1. Calculate the net proceeds of the issue after deduction of commissions, fees and expenses.

2. What is the all-in cost of fixed-rate funds to ECB, calculated as an internal rate of return?

3. Three-year government bonds yield 8.635% semi-annually (actual/actual). The swap spread is 85/88. What rate could ECB expect to be paid by a market maker on an annual 30/360 basis?

4. What is ECB's effective cost of floating-rate funds?

1. The issue price is 101.375%.

Deduct management and underwriting fees and the selling commission which total 1⅜%:

$$101.375\%$$
$$\underline{1.375\%}$$
$$100.000\%$$

We can now calculate the proceeds of the issue after expenses:

$$100\%*150,000,000.00 = 150,000,000.00$$
less expenses of 50,000.00
leaves proceeds of 149,950,000.00

2. To calculate the all-in cost we need to determine the borrower's cash flow:

year 0	−149,950,000
year 1	14,250,000
year 2	14,250,000
year 3	14,250,000
year 3	150,000,000

The redemption amount is the face value of the bonds.

To calculate the coupon payments, multiply the redemption amount by the annual percentage coupon:

$$150,000,000.00*0.095$$
$$= 14,250,000.00$$

To calculate the IRR on an HP12C, 17B or 19B, take the following steps (in any order):

$$149,950,000.00 \text{ CHS PV}$$
$$150,000,000.00 \text{ FV}$$
$$14,250,000 \text{ PMT}$$
$$3\, n$$
$$i$$

n	i	PV	PMT	FV
3	?	−149,950,000.00	14,250,000.00	150,000,000.00

To check data stored in any field press **RCL** and the required field:

■ e.g. RCL *n*

and the display should show 3.

The internal rate of return, on ECB's all-in cost of fixed-rate funds is 9.513%.

3. ECB would be able to receive the lower of the quoted prices so the semi-annual bond yield on the swap is the government bond yield plus 85 basis points or 0.85%:

> 8.635 s.a. actual/actual
> <u>0.850</u> s.a. actual/actual
> 9.485 s.a. actual/actual

Converting 9.485% from a semi-annual basis to an annual rate produces 9.7099%:

		DISPLAY
f	CLx	0.0000
9.485	ENTER	9.4850
200	÷	0.0474
1	+	1.0474
2	yˣ	1.0971
1	−	0.0971
100	×	9.7099

so the annual swap rate is 9.71% (30/360).

> **There is no market convention for converting from actual/actual to 30/360. In a full year the 2-day counts are equal.**

4. To calculate the approximate sub-Libor level convert both the all-in cost (9.513%) and the swap receipt (9.710%) to a semi-annual money market basis (actual/360):

p.a. 30/360	s.a. 30/360	s.a. act/360
9.710	9.485	9.355
9.513	9.297	9.170
0.197	0.188	0.186

So if ECB chose to receive 9.513% p.a. 30/360 rather than 9.710%, it could reduce its floating-rate payments to 6-month Libor less 0.18%.

EXPORT IMPORT BANK

Guarantor	State
Amount	150 million
Maturity	5 years
Coupon	9¾%
Issue price	101⅝%
Amortization	Bullet
Call option	None
Listing	Luxembourg
Denominations	5000
Commissions	1⅞%
Expenses	125,000
Swap	Into floating-rate funds (6-month Libor)
Negative pledge	Yes
Cross default	Yes
Pari passu	Yes

A better performer than the NKB, the lead picked a stable market and kept co-manager commitments down to 2 million. Nevertheless, demand was already beginning to thin. The deal was considered fairly priced at 15 basis points over the curve, and tightened in a couple of basis points before the government rally. Japanese demand underpinned the issue but some houses still did not find placement a foregone conclusion.

Questions

1. Calculate the net proceeds of the issue after deduction of commissions and expenses.

2. Calculate the issuer's all-in cost of fixed-rate funds.

3. The 5-year government bond yield is 9.49 (s.a. actual/actual) and the swap spread is 23/21. Calculate the rate at which the borrower could deal in the 5-year swap on an annual bond basis (p.a. 30/360).

4. Calculate the borrower's approximate cost of floating-rate funds.

1.

Issue price 101.625%
less commission 1.875%
= 99.75 %

99.75%* 150,000,000.00
= 149,625,000.00
less expenses of 125,000.00
= Net proceeds
= 149,500,000.00

149.5 **CHS PV**
150.0 **FV**
14.625 **PMT** (150.0*9.75%)
5 n
i

n	i	PV	PMT	FV
5	?	−149.50	14.625	150.00

All-in cost = 9.838
or
99.667 **CHS PV**
100.00 **FV**
9.75 **PMT**
5 n
i

n	i	PV	PMT	FV
5	?	−99.667	9.75	100.00

All-in cost = 9.838

3. The semi-annual swap spread is g+21 which is 9.70 semi-annual actual/actual

9.49 s.a. actual/actual + 0.21 s.a. actual/actual = 9.70 s.a. actual/actual
which is equivalent to 9.935 (p.a. 30/360)

4. The approximate difference between 9.935% p.a. 30/360 and 9.838% p.a. 30/360 expressed on a semi-annual money market basis can be calculated as follows:

p.a. 30/360	s.a. 30/360	s.a. act/360
9.935	9.700	9.567
9.838	9.607	9.476
0.097	0.093	0.091

So the borrower could pay 6-month Libor minus 9 basis points.

ASIAN INVESTMENT BANK

Amount	200 million
Maturity	7 years
Coupon	9¼%
Issue price	100¾%
Amortization	Bullet
Call option	None
Listing	Luxembourg
Denominations	5,000, 50,000
Commissions	1⅞%
Expenses	60,000
Swap	Into 6-month floating-rate funds
Governing law	English
Negative pledge	Yes
Cross default	Yes
Pari passu	Yes

The pricing of the deal at about 41 basis points over the curve at launch was generally considered fair, if a little on the bullish side. AIB said it received more aggressive bids on the deal, but not on the swap.

Questions

1. What is the borrower's all-in cost of fixed-rate dollars?

2. AIB wants to borrow floating-rate dollars at Libor minus 40 basis points. What swap rate is needed for the borrower to reach its target?

3. What is a negative pledge? What is a cross-default clause? Why are the bonds listed? Why the Luxembourg Stock Exchange?

1. An issue price of 100.750% less commissions of 1.875% leaves proceeds of 98.875%:

$$98.875\% * 200,000,000.00$$
$$= 197,750,000.00$$
Less expenses of 60,000.00
$$= 197,690,000.00$$

Year	Cash flow
0	−197,690,000
1	18,500,000
2	18,500,000
3	18,500,000
4	18,500,000
5	18,500,000
6	18,500,000
7	18,500,000
7	200,000.000

All-in cost = 9.483

2. To calculate the swap rate convert the all-in cost and the sub-Libor level to a s.a. bond basis and annualize their sum:

p.a. 30/360	s.a. 30/360	s.a. act/360
9.483	9.268	
	0.406	−0.400
9.908	9.674	−0.400

So a swap rate of 9.908 p.a. 30/360 would enable the borrower to generate funds at Libor minus 40.

3. A negative pledge is a promise by the issuer not to improve the security of other bond issues to the detriment of holders of this issue. Most international bond users are senior, unsecured, unsubordinated obligations of the borrower and a negative pledge is designed to offer investors assurance that they will not be disadvantaged at a later date. This is a standard convenant in international bond issues.

A cross-default clause ensures that if a borrower defaults on one transaction then that constitutes an act of default on all other transactions which have a cross-default clause.

If an issue is listed on a stock exchange then the bonds can be classified as "listed securities." This means that they can then be sold to investors who are permitted by buy only "listed securities."

The cost of a listing on the Luxembourg Stock Exchange is often very competitively priced and borrowers are usually keen to minimize the costs of issuing bonds.

POWERFORCE INC

Amount	200 million (increased from 100 million)
Maturity	7 years
Coupon	9½%
Issue price	101⅜%
Amortization	Bullet
Call option	None
Listing	Luxembourg
Denominations	5,000, 10,000
Commissions	1⅝%
Expenses	75,000
Swap	Into 6-month floating-rate funds
Negative pledge	Yes
Cross default	Yes
Pari passu	Yes

Launched at 40 basis points over the curve, the spread was maintained despite the difficult market conditions and traders described the issue as the best traded deal of the week. The lead manager took nearly half the issue, and reported broad institutional demand from the Middle and Far East, as well as Europe.

The initial 100 million of the deal was used to refinance PowerForce's mismatch floating-rate note due this year, but the additional 100 million represents new money for the borrower. The deal was swapped into floating-rate funds at a level of around 43 basis points under Libor.

Questions

1. What is the cost of fixed-rate funds to Powerforce?

2. What is the swap spread if the government bond yield is 8.812?

1.

Year	Cash flow
0	−199,425,000
1	19,000,000
2	19,000,000
3	19,000,000
4	19,000,000
5	19,000,000
6	19,000,000
7	219,000,000

AIC = 9.558

2. To calculate the swap spread, convert the all-in cost and the sub-Libor level to a semi-annual bond basis, add them together and subtract the government bond yield:

9.558 p.a. = 9.340 s.a. bond
plus 0.436 (43*365/360)
= 9.776 s.a. bond
less 8.812 (government yield)
= 0.964 = swap spread

EXPORT CREDIT

Amount	200 million
Maturity	3 years
Coupon	9½%
Issue price	101¼%
Amortization	Bullet
Call option	None
Listing	Luxembourg
Denominations	1,000, 10,000
Commissions	1⅜%
Expenses	50,000
Swap	Into floating-rate funds
Governing law	English
Negative pledge	Yes
Cross default	Yes
Pari passu	Yes

The pricing of this Triple A name was considered fair, but demand was slower than might have been expected, partly because of the Friday afternoon timing, ahead of a long weekend in London – traders manifested little desire to spend their holiday weekends worrying about positions. At 42 basis points over the curve, the pricing was reasonable, and the deal should perhaps have traded better. It remained within full fees, however, and should trade up further next week.

The deal was swapped into floating-rate US dollars, at around 55 basis points under Libor – better than market rates at the time.

Questions

1. What was the swap spread? The 3-year government bond yield is 8.722% semi-annually (actual/actual).

2. The present value of the mismatched cash flow is about 300,000 if we use a discount rate of 9.5599. What is the present value of the mismatched cash flow (119,800 p.a.) if the 1-, 2- and 3-year rates are 8.5, 9.0 and 9.5 respectively?

Answers

1. EC's cash flow is as follows:

Year	Cash flow
0	–199,700,000
1	19,000,000
2	19,000,000
3	219,000,000

All-in cost = 9.560%

EC would receive its all-in cost (9.560% p.a. 30/360) in the first leg of the swap and pay Libor – 55 in the second leg. In order to create funds at Libor – 55 the market price must have been 55 basis points (semi-annual act/360) higher than 9.560 p.a. 30/360. So if we convert each to a semi-annual 30/360 basis, we find that 9.90% is the price required to drive the issue.

p.a. 30/360	s.a. 30/360	s.a. act/360
9.560	9.342	
	0.558	0.550
	9.900	

If we subtract the government bond yield (9.900 – 8.7220) we find that the spread is about 118 basis points.

2. The present value of the mismatched cash flow is 302,494 calculated as follows:

	Amount	Rate	PV
Year 1	119,800.00	8.50	110,415.00
Year 2	119,800.00	9.00	100,833.00
Year 3	119,800.00	9.50	91,246.00
			302,494.00

AKB AUSTRALIA

Guarantor	AKB
Amount	150 million
Maturity	4 years
Coupon	9⅝%
Issue price	101⅞%
Amortization	Bullet
Call option	None
Listing	Luxembourg
Denominations	5,000, 10,000
Commissions	1⅞%
Swap	Into floating-rate funds
Negative pledge	Yes
Cross default	Yes
Pari passu	Yes

Probably the weakest of the Australian deals, AKB was handicapped by being the third 4-year issue and had to compete against IDB and Export Credit at five years. Swap traders said there was a better payer at four years, which may have prompted the decision. The general opinion was that this proved one bank name too many, although the spread looked reasonable at 58 over the curve.

Questions

1. What sub-Libor level would AKB pay if the swap price was $g + 87$ (against 6-month Libor) and the government yield is 8.75% s.a. (actual/actual)?

2. Calculate the net fixed-rate cash flow if AKB paid a sub-Libor level in return for a gross swap payment of 9.703%.

3. What is the present value of the mismatched fixed-rate cash flow?

4. What impact does the difference between this amount and 375,000 have?

1.

Year	Cash flow
0	−149,625,000
1	14,437,500
2	14,437,500
3	14,437,500
4	164,437,500

$$AIC = 9.703\%$$

$$Swap = g+87 \text{ s.a.}$$
$$= 8.75+0.87 \text{ s.a.}$$
$$= 9.62\% \text{ s.a.}$$
$$= 9.851\% \text{ p.a. } 30/360$$

The difference between the all-in cost and the swap receipt can be calculated by converting 9.851% and 9.703% to a semi-annual actual/360 basis to produce 6-month Libor minus 14 basis points.

p.a. 30/360	s.a. 30/360	s.a. act/360
9.851	9.620	9.488
9.703	9.478	9.349
0.148	0.141	0.139

So AKB pays Libor − 14 basis points.

2. Swap cash flow:

Year	Cash flow
0	375,000
1	14,437,500
2	14,437,500
3	14,437,500
4	14,437,500

$$150,000,000*9.703\% = 14,554,500.$$

This represents the gross swap payment.

If AKB elects to receive 14,437,500 in order to match the bond flow then the net cash flow is 117,000 p.a.:

$$14,554,500 \text{ less } 14,437,500$$

3. If the cash flow is discounted at 9.703%, it produces a present value of 373,271.28.

4. The difference will slightly alter the borrower's all-in cost of floating-rate funds.

APPENDIX 2
Glossary of terms

Accreting: An increasing principal amount in a loan or a swap.

All-in cost: The cost of funds in a bond issue after fees and expenses.

Amortizing: A systematic reduction in the principal amount of a loan (or a swap) over the life of a transaction.

Back-to-back loan: A variation of a parallel loan. Often used as a way of avoiding exchange control regulations. The structure of a back-to-back loan differs from a parallel loan in that the place of one of the companies is often taken by a bank which receives a deposit from a corporate client in one country and makes a loan to the corporate client's subsidiary in another country. It is sometimes used as a way of improving the situation which occurs when two parties enter into a parallel loan and have no right of offset. In a back-to-back loan the bank which makes the loan and its branch which takes the deposit are usually the same legal entity.

Basis point: One basis point is $\frac{1}{100}$ of 1 per cent, i.e., 0.01%. Some people talk about basis points "flat" and basis points "per annum." A basis point "flat" is a basis point in present value terms, or value today. One basis point per annum for five years, for example, means one basis point each year for five years and is obviously worth rather more.

Basis swap: A swap from one floating rate to another. Can be either a currency swap or an interest rate swap.

Bid: The price at which a bank is willing to pay a fixed rate of interest against a receipt of a floating rate, often 6 month Libor.

Bond basis: Interest calculation in which there are 30 days in each month and 360 days in each year. Many eurobonds use this as the basis on which interest is calculated. A bond basis could also involve a daycount which counts the actual number of days elapsed (actual/actual). This is the method used by the US Treasury for interest calculations involving US Treasury Notes and US Treasury Bonds.

Boxes and arrows: graphical representation of the direction in which payments flow between the parties to a swap transaction. They are also called "plumbing diagrams."

Circus swap: see **Cross-currency interest rate swap**

Commercial paper: Short term debt issued at a discount to its face value.

Coupon: The interest payment on a bond, paid by the issuer to a paying agent and then to investors.

Coupon swap: An interest rate swap, often from a fixed rate to a floating rate, or from a floating rate to a fixed rate.

Cross-currency interest rate swap: A swap from a fixed rate in one currency to a floating rate in another. Sometimes called a "circus swap."

Fixed rate: An interest rate which does not vary during the life of a transaction.

Floating rate: An interest rate which is reset at pre-determined intervals during the life of a transaction.

In-the-money: A position which has intrinsic value, i.e., one acquired at a rate which is more advantageous than current market rates.

Internal rate of return: The discount rate at which the NET PRESENT VALUE of a cash flow is zero. In the swap and the bond markets a borrower's all-in cost and an investor's yield to maturity are often expressed as internal rates of return.

Issuer: The borrower in a bond issue. For example a government, government agency, a supranational, a bank or a large corporate borrower.

Issuing house: The arranger of a bond issue and, often, of an associated swap.

Leg: one side of a swap transaction. For example, an interest rate swap might have a fixed "leg" and a floating "leg."

Libor: London Interbank Offered Rate. Theoretically the rate at which two AAA rated banks lend to each other in the interbank money market for loans and deposits.

Margin: The number of basis points above the US Treasury yield curve in an interest rate swap, often called the swap spread.

Money market basis: An interest rate calculation in which each year has 365 days (366 in leap years) over a base of 360 days, i.e., *365/360 or *366/360. Sometimes written as "actual/360" it is often used in the calculation of LIBOR payments, hence the name.

Net present value: The sum of future payments and receipts after discounting them to their value today. See **Present value**.

Notional principal: The amount used to calculate interest payments in an interest rate swap.

Off-balance sheet products: Prior to the introduction of Capital Adequacy in 1988 swaps had no regulatory capital requirement and banks limited the number and volume of their outstanding transactions by credit lines rather than balance sheet considerations. "Off-balance sheet" has now been replaced with the term "derivative," notwithstanding the view of some that swaps are not strictly speaking derivatives.

Offer: The price at which a market-maker is willing to receive fixed-rate interest against payment of US$ 6-month LIBOR.

Out-of-the-money: A position which has no intrinsic value, i.e., one acquired at a rate which is less advantageous than current market rates.

Payer: The party in a swap transaction which pays a fixed rate and receives a floating rate.

Parallel loan: An early version of a currency swap in which two companies lend to each other in two different countries. It is often used as a technique for avoiding exchange control regulations. Its principal weakness is that there are two unrelated legal agreements, often drawn up in different legal jurisdictions. There is therefore no right of offset in a parallel loan.

Plain vanilla: A swap with no unusual characteristics. A generic swap. Standard amount, maturity and payment.

Plumbing diagrams: graphical representation of the direction in which payments flow between the parties to a swap transaction. They are also called "boxes and arrows."

Present value: The value today of a future payment or receipt calculated by applying a discount factor.

Receiver: The party in a swap transaction which receives a fixed interest rate and pays a floating rate.

Spread or swap spread: The interest rate differential between an interest rate swap and the equivalent maturity US Treasury note.

Symmetrical risk: An opportunity where the downside risk is equal to the upside potential. Most financial instruments other than options demonstrate symmetrical risk profiles. If a transaction has a symmetrical risk profile then there is no financial requirement for one party to reward the other for entering into the transaction. The value of the two sides of the trade is equal.

Treasury yield: The yield to maturity on the most liquid US Treasury note which is nearest in maturity to a particular swap ("on-the-run").

Yield to maturity: The amount of interest, on an annual compound basis, which a bond would pay if held until redemption or the maturity date.

INDEX

Index